GRAHAM GOOCH

Ivo Tennant writes on cricket for *The Times*, *The Cricketer* and *Cricket World*. He is the author of two books, *Frank Worrell: A Biography* and *The Cowdreys*. He also writes on football, food and wine for various publications. Married with two children, he lives in London.

GRAHAM GOOCH

The Biography

IVO TENNANT

H. F. & G. WITHERBY

To
Carole, Camilla
and Tom

First published in Great Britain 1992
by H. F. & G. Witherby Ltd

First paperback edition published 1993
by H. F. & G. Witherby
A Cassell imprint
Villiers House, 41/47 Strand, London WC2N 5JE

A catalogue record for this book is
available from the British Library.

ISBN 0 85493 225 9

Printed and bound in Great Britain
by Cox & Wyman Ltd, Reading, Berks

Contents

Acknowledgements

It is a strange anomaly that in spite of Graham Gooch's pre-eminence and the fact that he has been playing Test cricket since 1975, there has not hitherto been a biography of him. His has been nothing if not a full career: runs, speculation and controversy have come in full measure. This book results from numerous interviews I have had with him down the years. I am grateful also for the help of his wife, Brenda (from whom he subsequently separated and who normally never gives interviews), and his parents, Alf and Rose, who likewise gave freely of their time and their photographs. The text was read through by a member of the Gooch family.

I am grateful also for the help of Stephen Green, curator of the MCC library at Lord's, and his assistants; and for the help of members of *The Times* newspaper and photographic libraries. Richard Wigmore's suggestions brought about many improvements, as was the case with my previous book, *The Cowdreys*. John Pawsey was, as ever, supportive throughout.

While I was at work on this book, John Arlott died. He had a great regard for county cricketers – and it struck me that this was for very good reason. Several of Gooch's team-mates, past and present, went out of their way to be helpful. I should mention in particular David Acfield,

John Lever, Alan Lilley and Derek Pringle. For an overview of Essex and Essex Man, the phenomenon he brought to a wider public, I am grateful to Simon Heffer, deputy editor of *The Spectator*. Alan Knott and Peter Roebuck were, as ever, fascinating company. Others were generous with their hospitality (and not one person asked for a fee). So, for their help, I thank: David Acfield, Terry Alderman, Mike Denness, Ted Dexter, Ray East, Frances Edmonds, Phil Edmonds, Peter Edwards, John Emburey, Keith Fletcher, Neil Foster, Angus Fraser, Mike Gatting, Alf Gooch, Brenda Gooch, Rose Gooch, David Gower, Simon Heffer, Doug Insole, Alan Knott, Alan Lee, John Lever, Alan Lilley, Bill Morris, David Norrie, Keith Pont, Derek Pringle, Clive Radley, Peter Roebuck, Graham Saville, Bobby Simpson, Mickey Stewart, 'Tiger' Surridge, Brian Taylor, Ian Todd, Bob Willis.

In preparing this biography I consulted the following books: *Batting* (Pelham, 1980); *My cricket diary '81* (Stanley Paul, 1982); *Out of the wilderness* (Collins, 1985); *Testing times* (Robson, 1991) all by Graham Gooch; *A cricketer's cricketer* (Unwin Hyman, 1989) by John Lever; *A peep at the Poms* (Arthur Barker, 1987) by Allan Border; *Another bloody tour* (Kingswood Press, 1986) by Frances Edmonds; *Captain's innings* (Stanley Paul, 1983) by Keith Fletcher; *Essex CCC: The official history* (Kingswood Press, 1987) by David Lemmon and Mike Marshall; *Frindall's score book* (Lonsdale, 1975) by Bill Frindall; *On the rack* (Stanley Paul, 1990) by David Gower; *Spinning in a fast world* (Robson, 1989) by John Emburey; *The Ashes retained* (Hodder and Stoughton, 1978) by Mike Brearley and Dudley Doust. And, of course, various editions of *Wisden*.

I.S.T.
January 1992 and September 1993

1

Essex Man?

Brentwood Leisure Centre. The very name implies a monument to the 1980s, to the boom years, to what the satirists would call the achievements of Essex Man. It lies in the heartland of the county, a golden triangle between Brentwood, Romford and Basildon, and even on a bleak evening out of the cricket season the management can count on support. For on the bill in the Centre's lecture hall is a man who is the very symbol of aspirations in Essex. Even at seven pounds a ticket, around five hundred people have come to hang on every word pronounced by Graham Gooch.

He is one of their own. Someone raised in that tract of suburban England where East London meets Essex; who for all his fame and wealth has not strayed from his roots and his devoted family. Earlier that autumn he had declared in a rare burst of emotion that, for all the pleasure he had derived from his success against the West Indies, Essex was his first love. Winning the county championship meant something else to this taciturn man whose every flowering, as cricketer, leader and human being, had been simultaneous. His fondest memory is not of victory at Sabina Park, nor of being asked to lead England in Australia, but of scoring a century that helped Essex win their first trophy, the

Benson & Hedges Cup, in 1979. 'He realised then, when he saw the tears in the eyes of the older players, what it meant to play for Essex,' said Ray East, his team-mate.

His achievements are recorded for posterity in *Wisden*, his ethos logged in the mind of everyone who has played under him, be it at county or Test level. After years of cliques, rifts and failures, Gooch, through his own personal form and leadership, the essence of which was that he would never ask anything of anybody that he would not attempt himself, had ensured England regained self-respect and self-belief. He combined a ruthless practicality with realism. He looked at his achievements cold-bloodedly, never letting a player smile when beaten; and he refused to concede that any cause was ever lost. His father put the correlation between captaincy and high scoring down to the extra responsibility he had been given: 'Graham has mellowed with age and has an inner drive to succeed at the job he is doing.' At the same time, his bearing, dedication and modesty were almost an anachronism.

When Gooch mounts the platform in the Brentwood lecture-hall, he does so to the warmest of applause. This being Remembrance Day, he wears a poppy as well as a tie. He is far from an establishment figure but is a stickler for certain standards, as more casual cricketers have found to their cost. He is seemingly more nervous than at the first of his series of cricket talks, even though that was at Cambridge. He is under the scrutiny not just of his neighbours but of his family, his then Essex chairman, Doug Insole, a close friend in Alan Lilley, and *The Times*. Yet once one or two jokes have met with the right response – 'Geoff Boycott would go to the mirror early in the morning and give a smile, just to get it out of the way' – his diction flows with an ease and clarity he would not have managed ten, even five years before. 'Brought up in soccer's imagery, he knows he has to avoid all those moons and parrots,' once remarked the *Sunday Times*. He does. At the end, his wife's aunt Grace declares that she never realised he knew so many rude words. In truth, though, this is set-piece humour: Gooch has acquired a fund of stories and jokes that would last for one and a half hours if he told each in turn. They served him well in the autumn of 1991 at cricket evenings and lucrative after-dinner speeches alike. Not the least admirable aspect of his pre-eminence in English cricket has been his determination to master roles which do not come easily to him.

For as astonishing as his achievements at an age when many of his contemporaries have already retired has been his own metamorphosis. 'If anyone had said when I played with Graham that he would become England captain, I'd have told them they were talking rubbish,' said Mike Denness, his first captain at international level. They played together for Essex until 1980, by which time Gooch was starting to take runs off the West Indies with a regularity – and occasionally lofty disdain – that no other batsman has been able to match since their awesome attack preyed on a batsman's physical shortcomings as much as on his technical limitations. Gooch's ability and courage were never in question, although his dedication once was. But his personality was an unknown element. In some respects, it still is.

This has something to do with an image that is so squeaky-clean as to be humdrum in an age when some sportsmen are featured prominently on pages of the tabloids that have nothing to do with sport. His cricket, which is dominant, does not reflect his character, which is essentially shy. 'People think we live glamorous lives, but that's not true,' said Brenda, Gooch's wife from whom he separated at the end of 1992 after sixteen years of marriage. 'Graham comes home from playing cricket, asks about the family and goes to bed at nine-thirty.' Home is his refuge. Gooch has many friends, but only three of them – John Emburey, the Middlesex and England spin bowler, Ken McEwan, the South African batsman who played for Essex, and Alan Lilley, also a former county colleague – are truly close. There is a bond between Gooch and Lilley that owes much to their East London working-class background. Lilley, who became the Essex Youth Development Officer and Gooch's personal coach, sees more of him away from cricket than anyone, yet will tell you that 'no one' knows Gooch 'other than himself'. Gooch is also close to his parents, Alf and Rose: in 1986, after years in which they had rented council property, he bought the house they now live in at Gidea Park, near Romford. 'Graham does not tell us anything about what he is doing,' said Alf, 'and it's not our way to ask. I don't know why David Gower has been left out of the England side.' Even Brenda, whose marriage to Graham endured throughout controversies and all his enforced absences, said that if she had not been at Chelmsford when Essex won the championship at the end of the 1991 season Gooch would not have breathed a word of this triumph.

Other friends – cricketers like John Lever, who played with Gooch for many years – find that something is still held in reserve. Keith Pont, who has known Gooch since they were in the same Essex Schools side, feels that this is the legacy of Gooch's decision to lead the first of the breakaway tours to South Africa in 1982. It was a decision which brought him the riches he yearned for, but at a considerable cost in other spheres of his life. 'As a joker, I used to be able to make Graham laugh,' said Pont. 'All of a sudden he was concerned with protecting his own back. He could only relax at players' parties, not in the pub, in case he was misrepresented. When John Emburey broke a finger in Cape Town on that tour, I shouted out from the crowd: "I'll play for half the money!" Graham didn't see the joke.'

There is no doubting that the opprobrium resulting from that tour – criticism from the media and Gooch's own father, vitriol through the post and down the telephone, the small autograph-hunter asking whether Gooch was the one who was a traitor – scarred him permanently. 'Being called a traitor ran deeper than he will admit now,' said Neil Foster, an Essex and England colleague. 'The whole affair changed us both,' said Brenda. 'Graham became more cautious; it takes a long time to get to know him now. But he sums up people well, although I prefer my judgement of character to his.' Gooch was twenty-eight when he decided, against the wishes of governments and cricket Boards of Control, to play in South Africa. He believes to this day that he did nothing wrong, that a sportsman should be free to play where he wishes. Naïve or not, stubbornly he stuck to that belief and, perhaps as a result, his personal performances were unaffected. The same could not be said of anyone else on that trip.

So his character became more inscrutable. His sense of humour and talent for mimicry that were so evident in his early years in the Essex side were camouflaged by suspicion. His eyes narrowed, his round shoulders inherited from his father grew increasingly hunched, and when the press came after him he retreated into a corner of the dressing-room or into the fastness of his family.

He looked sullen and miserable. Banned from Test cricket for three years, he was bored with batting on the county circuit and even more bored once he was out. He became socially isolated. 'A lot of people say he changed,' said Pont. 'He has grown away from some individuals with whom I thought he would remain friendly.'

That Gooch went to South Africa at all owed as much to his financial insecurity as to his disillusionment with Test cricket. His background was a poor one. His first home was a council flat in Leytonstone, a suburb that few have chosen to celebrate. His father was ultimately made redundant, as was Gooch when, having left school with six CSEs (like John Major he has forgotten the details), he embarked on a training in toolmaking. Not unnaturally, money has always held a particular importance for him. When his sister, also called Brenda (her husband, a compositor, was likewise made redundant), was training to be a hairdresser, she asked him to be her model. He refused. She offered him a pound. He accepted. Ever since, the sums he has earned have risen commensurate with his status, and his status since becoming captain of England has been as high as any sportsman. He plays for Essex not as their employee but as Graham Gooch Ltd. He has been lucky in his county (and they of course have been lucky in him): they realised he would be better off paying corporation tax on all his earnings, putting his expenses against his business (himself) and paying income tax on the salary his business pays him. Like many leading sportsmen, he earns considerably more through his activities off the field than he does from playing for his county and country. But he, more than anyone, was all too aware that he would not be England captain for ever and hence would not be accruing more than £100,000 a year for ever, either.

He pursues the accumulation of wealth with all the diligence that he brings to batting. He regretted that his state education had not run to classes on public speaking, on how to marshal and express thoughts, so he has worked on it himself, seeking professional advice. 'I think children should be taught to believe in themselves and their abilities, not to have negative thoughts but to take a positive attitude. If you have been bowled out by someone ten times, you must not think: Here comes the eleventh time. You've got to say to yourself: The law of averages says this time he won't do it.' Self-improvement is the key. When Texaco offered England cricketers television familiarisation courses in 1991, Gooch was one of the first to put his name forward. He is meticulously organised in all he does. When he arrives at, say, a dinner at which he is speaking, and the invitation is 7.30 for 8, he will be there at 7.55. He does not waste time; and he certainly does not waste time needlessly drinking, which might impair his concentration.

In his dedication, his belief in self-reliance and hard work – it is difficult to imagine any cricketer has ever been fitter – Gooch mirrors the aspirations of his own kind. His father, as with many who belonged to the London overspill into Essex, was originally a socialist: Gooch, as with many of the offspring of that generation, was a convert to Thatcherism. So, too, was his wife, whose family in a neighbouring suburb to Leytonstone were working-class but property-owning. Graham is not boorish, nor does he conspicuously display his wealth in a tribal manner, but in socio-economic terms he exemplifies those who without any advantages have improved their standing through high earnings. He has done so without any great motivation at school. One of Gooch's reports read: 'If he tried harder he could be a successful office boy.' He started at the bottom: the equivalent in cricket of beginning in the City as an office boy who was required to make the tea. He was the sort of person who could be relied upon if promoted from the ranks: Geoffrey Moorhouse, the writer, described him as 'descended from some sergeant in Victorian times who served Queen and country valiantly on the dangerous north-west frontier'. His outlook is in keeping with that. 'Mrs Thatcher did what she thought was right, and I respect her for that. It was good for the country,' said Gooch. 'I am a Conservative voter but I am concerned at the way a lot of public services have been cut and feel fortunate my family would not have to suffer at the sharp end of hospital waiting-lists. Labour seem not to be able to manage their budget, but the real trouble with politics is that seventy per cent of the time is spent arguing about what the other party would have done.'

The Pooterish bank clerks made their modest pile before the war. Essex Man, a predator on the cutting edge of the free market has made his money more quickly. The material ambition of used-car dealers and the self-employed in the retail parks at Basildon and West Thurrock stem from their bleak monotonous countryside, which has never attracted the establishment. The first great expansion out of London was to Ilford, Leyton and Barking, where the housing was cheaper and more shoddy than in Putney or Blackheath. John Major's perceived classless society and his consensus politics are not to the liking of thrusting, go-getting Essex Man; but his county, strategically placed for Europe, is a primitive backwood no more. This is reflected in the potency of the county's cricket: Essex supporters have become as hard as their Yorkshire counterparts in the days of Holmes and Sutcliffe. This by-product of commercial life has meant there is an element in the crowd at Chelmsford that is arrogantly intolerant of defeat. Friendliness and jollity have been sustained by the euphoria of winning. Essex County Cricket Club has been supremely well run during Gooch's time; but should their remarkable run of success come to an end – 1993 was not a successful season – the club is likely to suffer the same seismic upheavals as did Yorkshire.

Gooch's pride in his county and his club is not often to be found in a cricketer from any other part of the country. He is, above all, a totally self-motivated man. Other counties would pay him more, but he has no wish to play for them. He would not wish to live anywhere else. The *Sunday Telegraph* in a feature in 1990 charged the Gooches with being 'completely immobile in terms of taste, although they enjoy their prosperity', but Lynch Bages, the fifth-growth Pauillac, a present of which is the way to Gooch's heart, emphatically did not feature in his life in Leytonstone.

Much of the money he has earned from cricket has been invested in property: his house, the six-bedroomed stockbroker-style house in Hutton that he relinquished when he left Brenda, the house he bought for his parents, and a villa in Portugal for holidays. He does not know about the Stock Exchange and hence does not invest in it. He is keen to try most things once, but his ambitions have more to do with practicality and provision for his family than with self-education. 'I'm not very ambitious, I don't want more possessions,' said Brenda. 'But Graham is quite ambitious.'

Driving to a match at Lord's one day in the 1980s, Gooch was asked by David Acfield, the Essex off-spinner, what he intended doing when he retired from cricket. Gooch looked at him and said: 'Nothing.' It was a time when he was accruing money in large sums – from South Africa, a record Benefit, a libel action against the *Sun*. By the time he does retire, having had a second Benefit, doubtless he will have made enough money not to have to work again. Yet he is not an idle man. 'Graham would want to put something back into the game for the lifestyle he has had, for which he is grateful,' said Lilley. The chances are that he will retain his connections with Essex, possibly in the role of coach-cum-mentor that his friend and former captain Keith Fletcher occupied after retiring. 'Ken Barrington told me coaching was the next-best thing to playing,' said Gooch, 'and I have made it known that I would like to remain in the game.' There will be opportunities to do some work in the media, as there are now for every outstanding cricketer, and to undertake more public speaking – something he is keen to do.

Gooch's goals, however, stop short of social preten-sions. 'He is not at all ambitious in that sense,' said Alf. He has no intention of sending his three daughters, Hannah, Sally and Megan, to private schools. This is not because he cannot afford it – he can – but because he feels all children have the right to an education without having to buy one. There is a Church of England primary school in Shenfield and three state secondary schools in the area. 'I would never consider boarding schools because I would want my children with me,' said Brenda. 'It would break my heart to be parted – I don't even like going away for a weekend from them. My mother and father never left me. If we went anywhere, it was always as a family. They never had much of a social group, and I didn't like leaving them.' Gooch's disregard for social climbing was vividly illustrated when he was invited, along with all of his England side, to Buckingham Palace in the summer of 1991. He was primarily concerned that Alf, whom he was going to drive home later that day, should be allowed farther than the Palace gates. The Queen's Private Secretary relented, and very soon Alf himself was meeting the Queen. No longer does Gooch feel inhibited on such occasions. He has made his mark, and without changing his accent, although his voice is not as high-pitched as once it was. He has impressed no one so much as his father. 'My greatest pleasure is seeing Graham go up all the grades, and the way he has carried himself amazes me,' said Alf. 'I'm amazed with how he has dealt with people up the social tree considering he's not an educated lad, unlike David Gower, who should be able to cope with anything.'

If Gooch is happiest amongst his own in Essex, then he is not alone in that. 'Above all he likes very straight people,' said Emburey. He is wary of intellectuals and snobs, and particularly dislikes poseurs. He is not a racist – Monte Lynch, who is from Guyana, described Gooch's welcome when he first played for England in a one-day international as 'world class' – but he does not appreciate the strutting gait of some West Indians. One of their fast bowlers who made faces at him following three successive bouncers in a county match – none of which troubled Gooch – was seen off with a volley of abuse. He does not let taunts pass him by. The comments made by Lester Bird, the Deputy Prime Minister of Antigua, on England's 1986 tour of the West Indies still rankle. Gooch still resents the way he was received there and regrets the fact that he ever put his name to a statement by the Test and County Cricket Board declaring that he had no intention of playing against South Africa again. He remains especially wary of one former chairman of the TCCB and critical of any amateurism that he perceives as pervading a professional sport. He himself has worked hard at gelling the National Cricket Association with Mickey Stewart, England's former team manager. 'We don't like Oxbridge cliques with power bases because the game was not always run well in the past,' said Emburey. Nor does he respect journalists who do not have a knowledge of cricket, who reel off questions without asking whether he minds being interviewed or who compare him with captains from the past. 'These blokes like E. W. Swanton say you will never be a good captain unless you have been to a public school,' he muttered once. He finds it hard to cope with banal questions at press conferences, in part because of a low threshold of tolerance, in part because of his modesty. A female reporter asked how he felt after making his first Test century in Australia. 'All right,' he said, which put her down. Unless at ease with the person with whom he is working, the result is not productive.

He can harbour grudges, although not usually for long. He remains friends with Gower, in spite of feeling let down by him on England's 1990–1 tour of Australia. Gower's suicidally lackadaisical shot at Adelaide and his escapade in a Tiger Moth were responsible for this, though his merry-making with Allan Lamb hardly helped. After Ted Dexter had compared Gooch to a wet fish and then passed him over for the England captaincy without giving him an interview, Gooch pulled a face when Dexter asked the team to rally round Gower. Three years later no one was more complimentary about Gooch's batting and captaincy than the *Sunday Mirror* columnist turned chairman of the England Committee. For Gooch had effectively saved Dexter's job, as he had that of Mickey Stewart (who had been party to taking the captaincy away from him initially) – and both jobs were salaried. It was not Gooch's way to take the credit. They got on well, even if Dexter's relationship with his captain was distant – necessarily so, in Dexter's opinion.

Indeed, few do not get on with Gooch. He is much liked by his fellow-cricketers, at home and abroad. They see him as incapable of dissembling. 'He is earnest and honest, won't try to hoodwink you and means what he says,' said Derek Pringle, another Essex and England colleague. 'There are not many like that.' In England, only two players are known to dislike him, both of them well established. They are jealous of his achievements. Criticism of Gooch, if it is not of the Frances Edmonds brand, who cattily compared Gooch's IQ with his batting average in the Caribbean in 1986 – not surprisingly, they spent the tour on opposite sides of the swimming pool – has mostly centred on his stubbornness and naïvety. In an international batting challenge at the Oval in 1979, Gooch thought he had won when he passed the total of runs amassed by Clive Lloyd. He began to walk off, even though the rules stated Lloyd could still win, depending on how many times Gooch was out during the required number of balls he had to face. Brenda, who was in the crowd, told him he hadn't in fact won and should go back out. In the event he returned to the crease only after consulting his parents.

Is Gooch a happy person? If the effect of alcohol is to strip away the façade of an individual to reveal his true nature, then Ray East, the comedian, is a morose man and Gooch, the repining introvert, is gregarious. It has long been evident to those within the game that he is a nicer man than his own public pose has allowed. That is because he has not adopted any public relations. 'Our family does not like a lot of mush,' said Alf. 'We don't like blowing our own trumpets. We don't go seeking the limelight; but if it is there we'll bask in it, I can tell you.' The upshot of Gooch's success has been self-confidence and self-fulfilment. Now he can treat his dealings with the media, which has expanded rapidly even since Denness's time, as something of a game. 'Otherwise', said Lilley, 'it would finish him off.' On England's 1990 tour of the West Indies a journalist told him to cheer up. 'I'm OK,' said Gooch. 'But I've got to keep up appearances, haven't I?'

2

Leytonstone Boy

Indisputably, the Gooches are working-class, and they are proud of it. They are proud of the mutual dependence of their family, of the county they live in. There is a clannishness about East Enders: they stick together. 'Graham used to feel inhibited by his background in that he was only one step removed from being a cockney,' said John Emburey, his dearest cricketing friend. 'But it gave him strength of purpose and strength of character.' Another of Gooch's small group of close friends, Alan Lilley, will tell you that his drive to succeed also comes from his father. Alf Gooch is a man who by his own admission does not like anything to get the better of him. 'I think: Sod it; I'll get there in the end,' he said. 'And if Graham has got something in mind, then he will get that done.'

The origins of Gooch's talent for games can also be traced to his father, a keen and (in his youth) competent amateur sportsman. Sport is not otherwise a thread that runs through their family. Alf's father, an engineer in the merchant navy, was not sports-orientated. Alf's wife, Rose, whom he met in a dance-hall just before the Second World War, is from an East End family of publicans who similarly had no interest in sport. She worked in a wire-making factory either side of the war. Later she did attend matches in which Alf was participating. She helped make teas and in time wheeled her two children round grounds in prams, but her enthusiasm for sport remained fettered until her only son made it his career.

Alf played cricket and football as a schoolboy for West Ham Boys. When he moved to Oxford he played Isthmian League football as a goalkeeper for Oxford City and then switched to the forward line for Witney Town. This kind of flexibility was inherited by his son. When Alf returned to London he played club cricket for East Ham Corinthians on private grounds. In newspaper articles on the family he is labelled a carpenter, not least by his son, but his job with John J. Dunster & Sons in Hackney went beyond that: he was in charge of a section of the firm that bought materials for radio and television cabinets. His enthusiasm for DIY has never left him. In his seventies he often decorates and renovates the semi-detached house his son bought for him and his wife. He is keenly aware of the value of maintaining property.

Leytonstone was for political purposes a ward of Leyton when Alf and Rose lived there after the war. Their daughter, Brenda, was born in 1947. When, six years later, they had a son, lack of space necessitated a move. They had been renting half a terraced house in James Lane and moved up the road to Mills Court, a block of council flats. The family was not well off. For some time they did not own a car. Holidays were taken near to home, at the seaside at Romney or on the Isle of Wight. On the beach, on Wanstead Flats, a playing-field adjacent to home, and in the playground outside Mills Court, Gooch learned how to play cricket. 'Mum had lots of friends there and also knew it was good for us kids,' he said. 'There was no traffic danger, and I'd spend hours and hours whacking a ball about. Even when we went to the seaside, Mum would make sure the cricket bat got packed first. Mind you, when we got to the beach I used to have to wait patiently for my turn while she hammered the ball over the heads of dozing sunbathers.'

Of greater concern to Rose was her son's diet. As he grew up, Gooch liked to eat with gusto sausages and chips, luncheon meat and chips, corned beef and chips. He did not want to know about greens. Not that that impaired his vitality. When he started as a five-year-old at a mixed-infants school, Cannhall in Leytonstone, he found he liked football as much as he liked cricket, and he was starting to play both games with equal facility. He captained the school at both. He was encouraged by his first cricket master, Leonard Hall, who lived to see him become England captain. Sport was all, or virtually all, for Gooch was a pupil of average ability by the time he moved on to secondary school at the age of eleven. 'Graham's reports always said that he could do better,' said Alf, 'but he didn't get into trouble. I can never remember laying down the law. He was an honest boy – that was the way he was brought up and the way we acted. I hate liars, which is not to say I don't tell a white one now and again.'

Neither Alf nor Rose was a pushy parent. They were not overly concerned with their son's reports from his secondary school, Norlington School in Leyton, though they wanted him to try harder in the knowledge that this would help him when he left. He went there when he was eleven, and enjoyed it. It was a single-sex school with – unusually – proper cricket nets in the playground. 'I suppose we were typical London boys, quite streetwise, but nobody was really bad. We got up to the usual things, but there were no drugs then. I tried cigarettes but didn't like them and have never smoked,' he said. 'We were caned. Mr Davies, a jovial fellow, would give you the ruler across your fingers. Mr Jones, another Welshman – there seemed to be a lot of Welsh teachers – who taught geography, kept a size eleven slipper in his desk. We called it "Bonzo", and it hurt. You accepted your punishment without complaint. Detention was more of a deterrent – you stayed in after school and wrote lines. We preferred the short, sharp punishment.' Discipline was inculcated: each school day began with a morning assembly, and there were religious lessons. Gooch is not a regular churchgoer, nor does he hold strong religious convictions, but he is keen for his own daughters to have a Christian education.

Woodwork, which was at the core of his father's career, did not interest him. He never made his own cricket bat. He favoured metalwork. Most of all, though, he preferred sport. As well as cricket and football he played badminton and would go fishing at weekends. His talent for cricket was already obvious: 'He had that little bit extra over other kids,' said Alf. The first reference to him playing organised cricket outside school was in 1965, the year when Chingford, Walthamstow and Leyton were joined to form a new borough of Waltham Forest. As a member of the Under-Thirteen Eleven, one of three representative sides, Gooch was mentioned as one of the three best batsmen. He was chosen for Essex Schools and, wearing that cap, played alongside his father for East Ham Corinthians (albeit only because they were short). Alf encouraged him, rather than pushing him, and so, too, did Douglas Kemp, a teacher at Cannhall who took cricket. 'From the age of eleven Graham was playing cricket virtually all summer and winter,' said Alf, who took him for coaching at the Ilford cricket school.

This was run by Bill Morris, a white Jamaican who

had played for Essex and whose assistant was the teenage John Lever, then an aspiring professional cricketer. 'I remember John saying he would like to have a bowl at this rather big twelve-year-old, who proceeded to hit him all round the school,' said Morris. 'Graham was a strong hard-hitting boy whom we found could also keep wicket and had a natural ability to swing the ball at a young age. He was also very shy and not easy to get to know, but he would bat for hours. He almost lived there and treated me like a second dad.'

Morris had been coached by Andrew Sandham, whose approach to coaching a talented batsman would be to close his eyes and imagine how Sir Jack Hobbs, his old opening partner, would have played a particular shot. Morris applied this to Gooch, although often he chose to leave well alone. 'I felt people did not like to be told too much. If Graham was going to score a half-century, it had to be within thirty minutes; if he was going to make a century, it had to be in seventy-five minutes.' Morris captained Ilford, then as now a strong club (in addition to Lever and Gooch, Stuart Turner, Lilley and Nasser Hussain also learned their cricket there), and kept a beady eye on Gooch as he progressed through their various sides. Such was his promise that he had still to play for Ilford's First Eleven when he was asked to play for the Essex Second Eleven at Northampton. He was only fifteen. Not that he was given much to do: he was put down to go in last and did not have to bat. His memories have more to do with being driven to the ground by the captain, Johnny Welch, in a Rolls-Royce, and that one of the least attractive county grounds appeared to him to be like Wembley.

Essex Schools awarded Gooch his 'county honours' in 1968, which led to his selection for London Schools

Cricket Association's tour of Zambia and East Africa in 1969. This was when he met John Emburey. (Among the benefactors who made this tour possible were Lord Mountbatten, the Reverend David Sheppard and West Ham Football Club.) Chosen as a batsman and an occasional wicket-keeper, Gooch made 244 runs in nineteen innings with a top score of 55 in even time in a two-day match against a club called Livingstone. Others were more successful, notably Grahame Clinton, who went on to play for Kent and Surrey. Five matches were won, six lost. To Emburey, who remarkably took 56 wickets at 14 apiece, Gooch was already good company. 'We shared a room by chance. He was a fitness fanatic even then and a bit of a Jack-the-lad who used to crack the ball.'

The *Recorder*, the local newspaper in Ilford, faithfully logged Gooch's early innings. It described his maiden century as 'superb'. This was made in 1970, was unbeaten, and helped Ilford Colts beat Shoeburyness and reach the Trevor Bailey Cup final for the third time. Chosen to open, Gooch reached his century with the last of five sixes. He was unbeaten on 24 when the cup was won through a surprisingly easy victory in the final against King Edward VI School, Chelmsford. He was selected for the South of England against the North at Edgbaston, making 11 and 17 batting at number six. The side, captained by Keith Pont, included other cricketers of the future in Clinton, John Barclay, David Graveney and Andy Stovold.

The following year, playing for Ilford's Second Eleven, Gooch made 157 against Old Parkonians, taking only ninety-eight minutes to reach his century. Then, batting with Morris, he shared the Second Eleven's biggest opening partnership for six years (167) in beating Winchmore

Hill. Gooch made 84. There being little difference in standard between the Second and the First Elevens, Gooch played for the First Eleven that same summer, 1971, when he had his eighteenth birthday. Against Westcliff-on-Sea, who included Trevor Bailey, he made 87.

'I did not have a lot to do with Graham's technique or his mental approach, which is difficult for young cricketers,' said Morris, 'although I was still coaching him when he played for England since the Essex players would spend the winter at the indoor school under Brian Taylor and Keith Fletcher. Even then he had an over-strong right arm, and that is what causes him to play across the line sometimes. Watching him now with his heavy bat I see how difficult it is for him to hook. He uses a shot of his own, a swivel shot, but I never see him wrap his bat round his head.' Gooch still keeps in touch with his old coach, who retired to live in Scotland.

In this period Gooch was demonstrating that his talent for football could have led to a different career. He played as a striker for several years for Old Fairlopians in the Southern Olympian League, a club with decent facilities, and also had a season for Mayfield, an Ilford & District team. He continued to play until the 1977–8 season, his last winter before touring regularly with England.

'The very fact that Graham had talent got him into the teams. It wasn't a case of "Dad played a good game for him",' said Alf. 'But I told him to mix in because he would never push himself forward. When instructions were given he was the last to ask questions, although he respected what was wanted.'

Gooch would take his father's advice. Alf knew his son had a sporting prowess; he knew, too, of the insecurities inherent in a sportsman's career. 'It was my idea that Graham should learn a trade. I said to him that if we could get him into a college, then let's do it,' said Alf. 'At the time he accepted that Dad knew best.' So, after leaving school just before his sixteenth birthday, Gooch started an apprenticeship in toolmaking at Redbridge Technical College through joining the Association of Toolmakers in Ilford. He was with them for two years before being made redundant. The Association of Toolmakers, which went bankrupt, was taken over by Goldring, a small factory close to his home in Leytonstone, who made stereo equipment and carried on his apprenticeship. He attended Havering Technical College on day-release, continuing his training until March 1974, when he joined Essex full-time. Although it transpired that owing to his own success he would never use his qualification, he does not regret doing the course or the time he spent away from the cricket field. 'I quite enjoyed it,' he said. 'It gave me a realism.'

Gooch undertook this trade with the full backing of the then Essex captain, Brian Taylor. 'How do you know you are going to be successful?' said Taylor; and Gooch, of course, did not know. Taylor did spot 'an obvious desire to get on' when he watched Gooch play in the county's Second Eleven, in Club and Ground matches and in the new under-25 competition on the occasions when Gooch could escape from his apprenticeship. He would play at weekends and use days of his annual holiday, which amounted to only two weeks.

In 1972 he was selected to play for England Young Cricketers in two representative matches. Against Combined Services he did not bat, having been put down at number nine. Against MCC he kept wicket and, batting first wicket down, scored 47. He had another chance to go abroad when he was chosen for an England Young Cricketers tour of the West Indies. The London Schools tour of East Africa had been the first time he went out of the country, and he had gained a taste for travel. By now he knew some of his fellow-players: Barclay was to captain the party, and Clinton would be vice-captain. The pen portrait in the official brochure described Gooch as 'a genuine all-rounder. He has been selected as the second wicket-keeper and otherwise will play as a batsman/bowler.' On the six-week tour he encountered two bowlers of considerable potential – a splay-footed Colin Croft and the exceptionally tall Joel Garner – in making 57 against Guyana Youth and 48 against Barbados Youth. He also scored 29 when they played Trinidad Schoolboys. John Ikin, the manager and former Lancashire all-rounder, named Gooch as one of three potential Test cricketers in the England party.

And yet Gooch still did not feel he would be good enough to play professional cricket. Consequently he had no great ambitions to pursue a living out of it. 'But Bill Morris kept encouraging me, and my father would administer well-timed rockets whenever I got myself out. Without all that good advice and encouragement I would never have made it. Being a shy person, I know what youngsters go through when they join a better club to improve their skills. They feel a little isolated yet they desperately want advice from those who seem not to care about them. I went through the same problem when I first played Club and Ground matches for Essex; I felt a little out of it but imagined that many of the experienced players thought I wasn't up to the required standard,' he wrote in *Batting*, a coaching book. 'I suppose all players are guilty of that kind of behaviour and I now try to make the young lads feel at ease when they come to the nets at Essex. Just a few words like "Hello, I'm such and such, where do you come from?" mean everything to a youngster who might not do himself justice because of his shyness.'

Essex took a different view of Gooch's ability. Indeed, after he had acted as reserve wicket-keeper to Stovold in the Caribbean it seemed possible that Gooch might succeed Taylor as Essex wicket-keeper. Soon, though, he was remarking ruefully: 'It's tough enough just as a batsman.' In addition, his size was against him. 'The problem was, he became too big to keep wicket,' said Pont. 'But his talent as a batsman was recognised straight away.' In 1973, Gooch concentrated on bowling medium-pace and took 34 wickets in addition to scoring 265 runs as Essex won the Second Eleven championship for the first time. *Wisden* declared that 'he showed fine all-round ability'. He would turn up at matches on a moped with his bat and gear strapped to his back. Keith Fletcher, who became Essex captain the following year, had first met Gooch when he was twelve. He found him so withdrawn that he would say to others at the club: 'Does he speak?'

Fletcher did not rate Gooch's wicket-keeping but saw he had that crucial ability, time in which to play his shots. As for his appearance, Fletcher thought it extraordinary. 'Those were the days of mods and rockers, and this awkward-looking lad with thick-soled shoes took some terrible stick from me and the other senior pros. He was naturally laid back, and until you came to know him you would have said he was half-asleep. When I looked at him on telly years later at a time when he was breaking records and doing such a fantastic job as England skipper I had a little chuckle to myself. But he wasn't really a mod or a rocker, just a shy cricket-crazy teenager, and like all great players he soon sorted out who to listen to. I think if he had played for certain other less-animated teams he might have turned out rather differently. As it was, he came to purvey some inspired off-the-cuff remarks in the dressing-room and impersonate accents and idiosyncrasies as well as anyone I have seen. He was a completely natural games-player, be it cricket, football, golf, darts or squash.' He once beat a world champion, John Lowe, at darts; and a plaque at the Tollygunge golf club, Calcutta, commemorates a hole in one.

In the summer of 1973, Gooch had not yet finished his apprenticeship and had still to sign professional terms, but Taylor felt he was ready for county cricket. 'Physically Graham looked so ungainly but he could adapt himself very easily because he had a natural eye for a ball,' said Taylor. 'Wicket-keeping was of the least interest to him, but I reckoned then he could play for England as a bats-man. I always felt that a boy who was brought into the side should not be put under pressure because it was awe-some to play in front of a large crowd, so we decided to put him in down the order. He was very pleasant and well mannered and was shy of publicity – but not shy in the dressing-room where he became the biggest mickey-taker. His parents brought him up in the right way, but I would not have his father involved. I had no truck with fathers at all. I had to correct Graham as I did all the young Essex players if they became too casual. I was a very straightforward fellow, and they knew where they stood.'

So Gooch was chosen for his first-class début in a match against Northamptonshire at Westcliff in July. Going in at number five in a side captained by Robin Hobbs, he made 18 in his only innings. On a pitch that helped bowlers of all varieties he was leg before to Bob Cottam. That was his one first-class match of the season. He also played in the Gillette Cup and some John Player League matches without conspicuous success. Often he was coming in at the end of the innings. 'He had this strength at a young age of being able to hit across the line,' said Taylor, 'and it could have been eliminated. But he wanted to play that way, and the conclusion of the coaches was to let him go his own way. I felt the art of coaching was to improve on natural ability, not to coach it out.' Gooch had an affection for 'Tonker' Taylor, and was fond of imitating him: 'Same batting order, better batting,' he would pronounce in a gruff voice at tense moments on tour. Taylor, who still lives in Essex and attends most of their matches – 'I am always very well received by Graham' – planted the germ of success at Chelmsford, a ground that was little more than a field when Gooch began his professional career. He also placed a strong emphasis on fitness and discipline. 'Graham was a strong character, not so gentle as Alf, and did not shirk from trying to do what he wanted. But he took my standards of discipline – he had no choice. He had to come to the ground in a collar and tie and be clean-shaven. Today, players look like tramps.'

Taylor retired at the end of that season, having left an indelible mark on an impressionable young man. Gooch signed professional terms with Essex for 1974, but with no guarantee of first-team cricket opted to continue to play for Ilford – not least because of the quality of their pitches. David Courtney, Ilford's captain, declared that 'Gooch has more talent than any player I have seen at his age. And his record speaks for itself. He had already made Ilford's first team by the time he was eighteen.' When, at Whitsun, Gooch made 173 in 140 minutes for Ilford against Wanstead, Peter Rogers, a former Wanstead captain, told the *Recorder*: 'I have seen some good innings in my time, but that was just about the best I can remember.'

Gooch joined the Essex staff at the same time as Keith Pont, who was thought to have a more glamorous future. A much more extrovert character, he had captained representative sides ahead of Gooch and had batted above him. It transpired that he had a weakness against fast bowling and would become a cricketer of only average standing; but in 1974 he and Gooch were considered such good prospects that Essex decided to release Graham Saville, one of their long-serving players.

This was poignant, for Saville and Gooch were cousins. Not that their respective mothers had found out that they were first cousins for a long while. They had lived in adjacent roads as children, near Leyton Orient football ground, but had discovered their relationship only by chance on the day that Gooch was first picked for England. Saville's mother had not known that Rose had married a Gooch.

Saville's progression to county cricket had been, he thought, easier than that of his second cousin. He had played for Essex Grammar Schools and Essex Young Amateurs, whose facilities were better than were those of Essex Schools. He had had a worthy county career. 'When I was released, one of the reasons given that we had these two young prospects, I became the club's assistant cricket secretary so I saw a great deal of Graham over the next few years.' He was called out of retirement in 1974 to play one last match – Essex still had a small staff – and it was one in which Gooch made a considerable impact. Gooch had not begun the season in the side. When he was included, he made a pair against Gloucestershire at Bristol, batting at number five. Perhaps fortunate to retain his place, he then scored 30 and 44 against Sussex and was chosen to play with Saville against Lancashire at

Old Trafford. It was a match to remember: he was out just six runs short of a maiden century.

'Graham batted brilliantly that day,' Saville recalled, 'not least because he was up against Peter Lever and Ken Shuttleworth, both England fast bowlers at the time.' The cousins soon struck up a good friendship. Thereafter Gooch was assured of regular cricket, although surprisingly he scored few runs in the forty-over game, to which his style of play was already well suited. He was left out when Fletcher returned from playing for England but was reinstated for the following championship match and made 71 against Glamorgan at Swansea. Clearly, his maiden century would not be long in coming.

It came, in fact, before the end of the season. Leicestershire had one of the stronger attacks on the county circuit, including, as they did when they played against Essex at Chelmsford, Graham McKenzie and Ray Illingworth. Going in at number five, Gooch batted in the second innings with that brooding power the Essex supporters were to come to savour so often. He made an unbeaten 114 with eight fours and three sixes to bring about victory by two wickets. His century came in 115 minutes. For the last match, against Worcestershire, which was spoiled by rain, he was promoted in the batting order to number four. In fifteen matches that season he had made 637 runs at an average of 28. *Wisden* had this to say: 'Gooch really blossomed in the last few weeks of the season. He still has some way to go to confirm his promise but certainly appears to be blessed with the ability to succeed.' Fletcher, as well as Insole, thought he was an England batsman in the making – and it was not long before they were proved right.

3

A Chastening Début

The invitation was peculiarly formal. The stiff white card invited G. A. Gooch to play in the first Test against Australia at Edgbaston in June 1975, with the caveat 'if selected'. He was twenty-one, the youngest batsman to be chosen for England since Colin Cowdrey made his début in 1954, and had still not played a full season of county cricket.

The very best cricketers are playing for England by that age. And the selectors, chaired by Alec Bedser, reckoned Gooch was that good. The original recommendation to them came from Doug Insole, whose connections with Essex were such that he first saw Gooch bat when he was fifteen. 'He had never had a coach as such and yet was obviously a good player,' said Insole. It was for his potential rather than for his form that he was chosen, although already he had made 75 and 12 for MCC against the Australians at Lord's. For their part, the Australians had realised they were watching a batsman in the making. Almost as soon as he had begun his first innings, Ian Chappell, their captain, went across to his great fast bowler Dennis Lillee and in his bombastic way suggested he should test Gooch's resolve. In that Lillee dismissed him in the second innings, he did. Yet the Australians remained concerned about Gooch to the extent that when he was selected for England a few days later his name featured prominently in their eve-of-Test team-talk. The gist was that they did not want him to play in too many Tests that summer and they were intent on undermining his confidence as soon as possible.

This was an exceptionally strong Australian side, far from the ideal opposition for Gooch to have encountered in his first Test. Put in to bat by Mike Denness, who was to become a team-mate of Gooch's at county level, Australia made 359. Gooch's recollections were, not surprisingly, of nerves even when fielding well away from the bat at fine leg: he was terrified of the ball coming to him and returned it to the wicket-keeper as swiftly as humanly possible. His recollections of batting are, not surprisingly, more vividly etched. No sooner had England's first innings begun than a thunderstorm burst over the ground. By the time play restarted, the uncovered pitch had been saturated. The ball reared off a length alarmingly. The conditions were quite bad enough without Gooch having the added burden of coming to the wicket when England barely had a run on the board.

The scorebook shows that he came in at number five at 6.23 and departed at 6.24, having faced three balls and not scored. It was a sacrificial innings: if a nightwatchman was contemplated, one was not used. Max Walker, obtaining lift through his brisk medium pace, dismissed him in that most unsatisfactory of ways: caught at the wicket down the leg side. The shot was more a tentative push than a glance. England were bowled out for 101 and, having followed on, were 93 for 5 by the close of play on the third day. This time Gooch went in shortly before lunch and survived seven balls. Again he had not scored when Jeff Thomson dismissed him, caught behind as in the first innings. The ball was a markedly good one, a fast leg-cutter which he probably did well to touch. Fletcher, who was batting at the other end, indicated as much as Gooch passed him on the way to the pavilion.

In the stands, Rose was watching, complete with new outfit and borrowed binoculars trained on her son. Gooch's selection had, her son reckoned, given her greater pleasure than anything else in her life. He had spotted her waving at him when he went out to bat a second time. 'Me, a poor lad from the East End, had been picked to play in the company of men who'd virtually been born to wield a cricket bat for their country, and she was bubbling like never before.' Neither she nor Alf has mentioned the match to their son to this day. They knew at the time there was no point in offering advice.

Wisden does not detail players who have recorded a 'pair' on their Test début, through shortage of space rather than through the kindness of the editor. Gooch knew, though, that everyone else knew without having recourse to record-books. It put his game back by three years in that he had to wait that long before he was chosen for England again. It affected, too, his sense of insecurity, which surfaced when he opted out of Test cricket to play in South Africa. Even when he appeared on 'This Is Your Life' fifteen years later he found the dreaded footage had been retained. Yet Insole, Denness and Fletcher remain in agreement: the decision to select him was the correct one. Fletcher has no doubts that had he been retained throughout the four-match series he would have justified his selection. As it was, he was chosen for just one more Test.

Denness himself was sacked and replaced by Tony Greig at Lord's; Gooch was to go in again at number five. In better conditions he made 6 and 31, and by his own admission batted badly. On the first morning he was one of Lillee's victims in another collapse, caught again by Rodney Marsh off a defensive push. In the second innings he was uncharacteristically cautious. In spite of striking four fours he rarely felt that he was hitting the ball in the middle of the bat. His dismissal, after facing seventy-one balls, was curious: Ashley Mallett bowled him as he attempted to cut a yorker that pitched on middle and off. There was to be no third chance. Other countries might have given him a further Test or two, but not England.

The selectors sent Gooch back to county cricket, doubtless knowing full well that his time would come again. 'I knew he would work hard at his game,' said Fletcher. Yet for the remainder of the 1975 season his form fell away completely. Although he made 1,000 runs in first-class cricket for the first time, not many of them were scored after the Lord's Test. It was not until the winter that his confidence returned in an atmosphere that was less fraught. He played club cricket for Green Point at Sea Point in Cape Town, where he drank in the sunshine, the scenery and the country on a trip that was precursory to more contentious visits. During the week he worked in a sports shop in the centre of Cape Town.

He took with him his fiancée. Brenda Daniels, the daughter of a motor mechanic, came from the same tract of East London. Chadwell Heath is but one of many suburbs in the urban sprawl on a main line out of Liverpool Street: blink, and you will miss it. Brenda had started going out with Graham when she was eighteen, a year his junior but a more forceful personality. 'She doesn't stand any rubbish,' was how Keith Pont described her. 'Brenda says what she thinks. If Graham was getting out of line, she'd soon tell him,' said Keith Fletcher. Like

Gooch she was straight as a die and Essex to the core. Clive Radley, who befriended Gooch on his first tour, calls her 'the salt of the earth'. Her love of dancing had taken her to the Ilford Palais where she had met Gooch and his friends from Redbridge Technical College. He, she said, hated dancing. 'He had two left feet.' The story goes that he nodded off on their first date, although that, she says, belongs to the make-believe of the humorists who shared the Essex dressing-room with Gooch.

Her experience of book-keeping for chartered accountants in the City and then for a shipping company in Barking stood her in good stead for helping Graham run his business affairs in later years. When they met, he was, she thought, extremely shy. 'He went around with a group of boys from Redbridge whom he no longer keeps up with, but he never found it easy to mix.' Two decades on, Brenda still went bopping – but Graham preferred his running.

They were married at St Chad's, Chadwell Heath, in October 1976. Gooch's brother-in-law, Keith Oldham, who was a compositor, was best man. Alas, the honeymoon in Blackpool was a disaster. 'We had spent every penny we had on buying a house which was in such a state that we couldn't live in it. We took three years to do it up with the help of both our families and other people's cast-offs,' said Brenda. 'In Blackpool it rained on the first day, and the second day I found I hated the place. I didn't expect every other shop to be fish-and-chips or selling kiss-me-quick hats.' Rather than stay there, they spent a night in the Lake District at a nicer hotel and promptly drove back to London. Nor did they remain in their three-bedroom terraced house in Chadwell Heath for longer than was necessary. Indeed, in eleven years they were to have five different houses.

Their second home, a three-bedroom house in Gidea Park (the area where Gooch's parents now live), was on a busy road with a bus stop outside. Worse, boys from a nearby school would set fire to the conifers Brenda had planted and taunt her when she stepped outside. That was enough for her husband. After eleven months they moved to another house in Gidea Park, this in a more quiet position. From there to Shenfield, or Hutton as it is appropriately known, and a newly built house that later was owned by Jimmy Greaves, the great footballer. Four years after that, following Gooch's Benefit, they moved once more, within the immediate area.

Brenda became a reluctant member of that select fraternity known as cricket widows. She knew before she married that her fiancé would almost certainly be away from home in winters to come, a state of affairs she naturally disliked but was prepared to tolerate. The attraction for her when Gooch led the unofficial tour of South Africa in 1982 was not so much the money as the fact that she could spend the winter with him, as she had done at Sea Point in 1975 and 1976. In her years of marriage to one of the best-known of English cricketers she was rarely recognised when shopping at Tesco and yet had to change her telephone number, turn reporters away from her door, put up with abusive telephone calls, stop reading vitriolic tabloid newspapers and make her own judgement on just who can be trusted. And, fearing for her husband's future when he retired from cricket, she was all too aware that a sportsman out of sight is out of mind.

At Chelmsford she would be found in the 'mole hole', as the area reserved for players' wives and their families is known. Gooch's parents like to sit in the open seating beneath the press-box. They attend virtually every match and have done so since Gooch first played there, quite content to sit with sandwiches and Thermos rather than flit in and out of the hospitality tents.

Their support meant much to Graham as he fought to regain his form in county cricket: 1,189 championship runs at an average of 44 in 1976, good enough for him to be chosen for the three one-day internationals against the West Indies. A decent score and probably he would have regained his Test place: 32, 5 and 3 were simply not sufficient to gain recognition. In 1977 he did not reach 1,000 runs and averaged a paltry 27. County opponents had, he surmised, sorted out his strengths and weaknesses and bowled accordingly. At one stage he was batting as low as number six, no place to build an innings owing to the hundred-over limitation that existed at the time. Almost as soon as he went in he had to start slogging.

There was a further reason why Gooch felt he was not batting well. His weight had gone up from 13½ stone to 14 stone during the 1977 season. Not surprisingly, he felt sluggish and unfit. At the end of that summer he decided to start running, which, coupled with playing football, meant that he was mentally and physically attuned for the 1978 season. So began a quest for fitness that he has pursued ever since, all over the world. Then, he would run for four miles three times a week.

In summer he would run round the ground before start of play. When he lived closer to Ilford than to Chelmsford, he would jog to the ground from home. Several Essex grounds are sited in public parks and consequently ideal for runs during a match. Disliking watching the play after he had been out, Gooch would often exercise instead. 'He never wanted to sit down,' said Radley. 'He would put his bat down quietly, unlike some other players, and go off and run or have a game of squash, even if he had been in the middle for two hours. He doesn't look like an athlete but he is very strong and fit.' Denness, for one, was astonished at the change that came over him. 'Graham is a totally different individual today from what he was when I joined Essex in 1977. He was laid back, slouched around the field, was a bit over-weight, and I thought he might end up as another Colin Milburn.'

Denness it was who was responsible for the other trans-formation in Gooch's cricket. Gooch himself had man-aged to overcome his sluggishness and lethargy at the wicket and yet was not being given the opportunity to play long innings. Ahead of him in the Essex batting order were Denness, Brian Hardie, Ken McEwan and Keith Fletcher, all of them accomplished batsmen. Denness suggested to Fletcher that Gooch be moved up the order at the beginning of the 1978 season, reasoning that he was having all too few opportunities to bat. His idea was put into effect from the very first match against Cambridge University, Hardie moving down to bat at number six. This was to be the making of Gooch, if not immediately. 'It was disastrous at first,' said Denness. 'Graham batted as if he was still going in at number five and never gave any sign of concern if he was out without scoring. He would be on the telephone to Brenda straight away. He wanted to be a Test player but didn't have the dedication to work at his game and didn't know where he was going. Keith Fletcher and I tried to get through to him that now he had two strings to his bow – he could open or bat down the order. He worked on his batting and his fitness, fat turned to muscle, and he was very much the player by 1979. He realised he could do it and that opening was the easiest place to bat if he could play the moving ball.'

Gooch also realised that opening tightened up his game and helped his concentration immeasurably. By Ilford week at the beginning of June he had become accustomed to his new role to the extent of making centuries in both matches, against Kent and Northamptonshire. In the second of these he made 129, putting on 321 for the second wicket with McEwan, who had become a close friend. Their partnerships together, the one bludgeoning his shots, the other all grace and timing, were perhaps the prime feature of Essex cricket in this period. That day they set an Essex record; but, beyond that, Gooch's innings led to his Test recall.

For his first Test match for three years, Gooch was to open. England were playing Pakistan at Lord's in the second of a three-match series, and significantly their success in winning had much to do with him and two others in his own youthful age group: David Gower and Ian Botham. Driving powerfully and excelling with the late cut – a shot he used with less frequency as the weight of his bat increased – he made 54, putting on 101 with Gower in ninety-seven minutes. In the third Test he scored only 20 but retained his place for the three-match series against New Zealand, in which he topped the batting averages with 190 runs and one unbeaten innings of 91 which led to England winning the first Test in another three-match series. 'With rain forecast and obviously imminent, Gooch cast care aside and launched a brutal attack,' wrote *Wisden*. His eleven boundaries were 'truly hit', as they have been ever since. He also played an innings of 94 in one of the two one-day internationals that won him the Man of the Match award. For Essex he averaged nearly 40 and clearly had booked himself on to the plane for England's tour of Australia.

Above all, Gooch was now a destructive batsman. He

was already using a heavier bat than the majority of players – 2 lb 14 oz as against the standard 2 lb 8 oz – with a thick handle and several rubbers around it. In time, that weight was to go up to 3 lb. To him, it felt comfortable in the pick-up as well as the grip, and there was more chance of hitting the ball hard, which was particularly important in one-day cricket. Technically, he was an orthodox batsman save for the shot he whipped to leg by playing across his front pad. He looked to implement this by hitting the ball not in the so-called 'sweet spot' but closer to the edge of the bat. So hard would the ball go that even off a thickish edge it would sail through square leg and, at Lord's, disappear down the slope to the boundary. Bob Willis would tire of bowling 'the nip-backer that would fly off a two-inch edge for four'. Gooch would cover the leg stump but would leave himself vulnerable to being lbw: on his first tour of Australia Rodney Hogg and Alan Hurst both dismissed him in this way and he was later to have his well publicised difficulties against medium-pacers of the likes of Terry Alderman. Otherwise, he would try to hit as straight as possible. If he was caught in the slips, as often as not it would be through moving too far across his stumps.

At this stage of his career he preferred to play off the back foot early in his innings. He did not concern himself overmuch with taking the short single to mid-on, and hence the fielder could remain a little deeper: Gooch would rather wait for the overpitched ball which he could hit to the boundary. Yet Clive Radley recalls that when they played together for England Gooch had consideration for a different type of batsman at the other end. 'For someone who scores a lot of runs in boundaries, he is always prepared to run for people like myself who score a high proportion of ones and twos.' He was brave and, once physically fit and accustomed to staying at the crease for long periods, could maintain his concentration. The correlation between mental and physical fitness had been little appreciated within the game before. He did not mean to treat bowlers with disdain, but there were times when he played spin with such ease that he would lose his wicket through carelessness. He and Mike Gatting, both exceptional players of slow bowling, grew up in the era of great West Indian fast bowling, which doubtless coloured their attitude when playing anything of lesser pace. David Acfield described his team-mate as 'a super crasher of spinners'. Unlike Fletcher, Gooch was not a great technician against spin; he was quick on his feet for a heavy man and simply shifted his weight from one foot to the other and hit through the line. He once told Phil Edmonds that there was no way he would get out to a left-arm spinner bowling round the wicket. 'If I went over, Graham would be more inhibited unless I was pitching the ball outside off-stump,' said Edmonds. 'I always enjoyed bowling at him.' Gooch played the two foremost English spinners of the day, Derek Underwood and John Emburey, particularly well. If the ball was turning, he aimed to drive Underwood over extra cover; if it was not, he played him as he would an off-spinner and looked to hit him over mid-wicket. He came to know Emburey and consequently his variations so well that ultimately John could hardly bowl at him.

This, then, was the batsman, of sound temperament and primarily back-footed, who went to Australia. He wore a helmet at all times, and had no qualms about doing so. He felt more confident and therefore a better batsman for it. If there was any trace of selfishness in his batting — and this was not discernible — it was a trait deployed for the good of the team. 'He will never be a

Boycott, never worry about making a century when the team comes first. Others have followed him because of it,' said John Lever, another good friend who was also on Gooch's first tour. Gooch was quiet off the field and sometimes appeared indolent on it, at any rate when he was fielding. His sun-hat, moustache, swarthy look and unhurried gait led Mike Brearley to nickname him 'Zapata'. The captain reminded him that such an impression, however deceptive, could affect others.

For reasons that Gooch could not fathom until he returned to England, he had a poor series; this in spite of learning the art of playing quick bowling off the front foot. He played in all six Tests, worked diligently in the nets with Ken Barrington, the assistant manager, was happy, and yet made only 246 runs. His only century on the tour, against a Western Australia Country Eleven at Albany, was not deemed first-class. Had the batsmen who were out of the Test team run into some sort of form, he would have lost his place. In the first two Tests he opened and made one score of 43 and three of single figures. Hence for the third Test (the only one England lost) he was placed at number four, where he made 25 and 40; in the fourth 18 and 22; in the fifth 1 and 18; and only came into form in the final match of a series England won overwhelmingly, scoring 74 at Sydney. Insole, who was managing the tour party and who felt Gooch was becoming over-critical, had had a word with him beforehand to impress upon him the need to stake his claim for the future.

Upon returning to England, Gooch swiftly discovered what was afflicting his batting. He had experimented altering his method in the nets with Barrington, who told him he could not focus on the ball properly since his whole body was moving. Keeping him away from the new ball by batting at number four had made next to no difference.

Barrington, whom Gooch greatly respected, had suggested he adopt a high stance similar to that used by Tony Greig, the bat raised in readiness for the ball, and he worked on this in the nets without putting it into practice on the tour. Gooch was convinced of its efficacy one evening when he watched video-tapes of his batting in Australia. An aunt of Brenda's, Mrs Grace Richman, who lived in Ilford, had recorded all of Gooch's televised innings, little realising how staggered he would be when he saw them.

'I had never seen myself like that before,' he said. 'It was like listening to yourself on a tape-recorder for the first time. I watched the tapes again and again and decided to alter my approach since I was staggered at the angle of my head and my crouched style. I wanted to concentrate on getting my head level.' He found he was becoming square-on, his chest facing the bowler as the ball was delivered. He was moving too far across the crease, and his head was dipping down into his body. The more he tried to concentrate, the worse his stance had become. 'I could not get my head up straight, my eyes level, and be comfortable in the conventional stance,' he said.

He promptly bought a video-recorder. He and his aunt between them could record an entire day's play and then swap tapes. At the start of the 1979 season, when Gooch first tried his new stance in the middle, he found some people were laughing at him. Certainly his backlift was more exaggerated than Greig's; and yet, not being as tall, he could come down on the ball more quickly. As his bat was already straight at the top of the backlift, it was not coming down across the line. Insole felt that he had a tendency now to play round the front pad, and there was no shortage of critics among older players. His father had – and still has – a telling comment for them: 'Just look at the scorebooks.' The stance, essentially sideways-on, became his trademark, one copied by countless cricketers and children the world over.

Whatever stance Gooch adopted, he remained an attacking player. In 1979 this was especially emphasised in one-day cricket. He made 838 first-class runs but almost 600 runs in seven Benson & Hedges Cup innings, culminating in a memorable century in the final that helped Essex beat Surrey and hence win their first trophy. It was the year, too, when they won the county championship for the first time. In the World Cup, Gooch had some success, making 53 against Australia and 71 against New Zealand, on both occasions winning the Man of the Match award, and scoring 32 at number four in an unfruitful assault in the final against the West Indies. He was chosen for all four Tests against India and came close to scoring his maiden Test century at the Oval. This was, uncharacteristically, a dogged affair. On the first day he made 79 in four hours and naturally felt confident of adding the necessary 21 runs the next morning. He was out in the first over to Ghavri. This followed an excellent two-hour innings of 83 in the first Test which ended with a flat-footed push at Kapil Dev. He put these lapses down to lack of concentration rather than to his temperament, which has never let him down. A medium-pace bowler was more likely to deceive him than one who banged the ball in short: Gooch liked the ball to come on to his cumbersome bat. Doubtless, too, there was a psychological reason: a maiden Test century was to be treasured.

For Essex, there were no such inhibitions. Gooch's century in the Benson & Hedges final remains his fondest memory in his career, which, considering his more recent achievements, shows just how much playing for his county means to him. It was the first century in any final of the competition and gained him lavish praise from *Wisden* for his astonishing alliance of strength and timing. Bowlers like Robin Jackman and Hugh Wilson were repeatedly picked up and dispatched over square leg. 'It was his masterpiece at Lord's which lifted him above the ranks of ordinary; which convinced everyone of his star status. With a mixture of frightening power and controlled fury, he not so much dictated to the bowlers as destroyed them,' wrote *Wisden*. His innings of 120 included three huge sixes and eleven fours. Gooch's prime recollection, though, is not so much of his batting as of the eruption that greeted him and Denness when they went out to open the innings. Everywhere they looked there was an Essex supporter. Gooch won the gold award, as he has continued to do with remarkable regularity. By the end of the 1991 season he had gained nineteen such awards, more than anyone else in the game.

In choosing Gooch as one of their five cricketers of the year, *Wisden* said that 'he has had to endure immense pressures on his way to the top; pressure that would have got the better of players not gifted with his fierce determination to succeed'. The sports writers dusted down their less felicitous phrases. Gooch bludgeoned, biffed, carved, clumped, hammered or just plain thumped bowlers. They noted that his dead-pan face never changed while he did so. On the field he gave vent to his emotions only through his impersonations of others – his mimicry of Bob Willis's ungainly run-up and action was admired even by Willis himself – which, sadly, were banned by the Test and County Cricket Board.

Both in the England and the Essex dressing-rooms he was much liked. Ken McEwan, Alan Lilley and John

Lever were perhaps his closest friends amongst his own county colleagues; for England, John Emburey became such an inseparable companion that other players referred to them as Hansel and Gretel. When they went shopping separately during one tour they came back with identical sweaters.

Humour and camaraderie kept Essex going. Gooch did his fair share of mickey-taking but did not always relish being on the receiving end. On one occasion at Ilford a corpulent supporter opened the dressing-room door, said to Gooch, 'I see you are still picking your nose,' and promptly left. Everyone but Gooch was convulsed, although he did eventually see the joke. He could be moody rather than dour and sometimes could not bring himself to absorb the comments of others; normally, though, he contributed as much as anyone to the jollity and he particularly appreciated Ray East's japes. His own sense of humour was essentially sarcastic. Standing in the slips one day, Gooch asked Emburey what he was doing during the winter. When told that Emburey was working in computers, Gooch said: 'You painting them?'

He had an ambivalent relationship with David Acfield. They saw eye to eye off the field but not necessarily on it since Acfield felt that when they played together Gooch did not understand the problems spinners faced. 'Graham was not inhibited because he had made his mark in life, but he might have had a bit of a social chip when he mimicked my public-school accent.' And yet they would dine together – Pont reckoned that subconsciously Gooch wanted to improve his diplomatic skills – and discuss wine. Acfield himself felt he might have been able to help Gooch in some ways. 'Neither he nor Keith Fletcher had any interest in talking to people who came up to them because neither felt it was a necessary part of being captain. Graham was always thinking: What's this bloke's angle?' But as he matured, Gooch became better able to cope with incessant questions and demands. Peter Edwards, the Essex secretary-manager, said he had never heard any criticism of him from members. 'I get very little reaction, which is a good thing since members are always quick to complain,' he said. Acfield, who became heavily involved in the administration of the club, said that Gooch would go out of his way to be polite to players' wives and would remember the names of their children. He enjoyed players' parties but would generally drink sparingly: two pints or glasses of red wine and he would be slurring his words or nodding off. David Gower felt that both Acfield and later Derek Pringle, another Cambridge graduate, helped Gooch develop in a different sphere. So, perhaps, did Gower himself. Gooch did not really understand him, but they became good friends, and in spite of subsequent differences have remained so. Of other England players, Gooch tolerated and respected Ian Botham for his ability, less so for his attitude; he hit it off with Geoff Boycott better than most, perhaps because Boycott recognised an equal. Normally the Yorkshireman was not one to impart much in the way of advice, especially to fellow opening batsmen; and yet Gooch has often turned to him for technical advice. Boycott reckoned Gooch adjusted notably quickly to opening; and the two men forged an understanding based on good humour when they batted together. 'Graham admires Geoff for the work he has put in on his game,' said Emburey. 'It has been a lesson to him, and he would like to be known for having worked as hard.' Gooch was less impressed with Boycott's vehement criticism of other players when he later became a television commentator.

They opened together against Australia on the hastily

arranged 1979–80 tour. Their different approaches complemented each other: Gooch forever looking for runs
and Boycott accumulating and wearing down a better
class of bowler than they faced the previous winter when
World Series Cricket claimed the likes of Dennis Lillee.
In the World Series Cup matches, played as hostilities
between cricket authorities and Kerry Packer ceased,
Gooch was surprisingly out of sorts, making low scores
relieved by 62 out of a total of 164 in one match against
Australia. His winter, though, was altogether more successful than that of the previous year. As before, he
worked hard in the nets and now topped both the Test
and the tour averages in spite of his surprising omission
from the first Test, where England opted to play three
spinners in Underwood, Willey and Miller. In the second
Test he made 18 and 4; then in the third 99 and 51.
Seeking his maiden Test century, he ran himself out in
the last over before tea and, returning to the pavilion,
said rather plaintively: 'I got that wrong, didn't I?' For
him, always the pithy comment rather than the histrionic
outburst. Yet this was the innings which established him,
quite firmly, as an international cricketer. England lost
the series, but he had won a reputation after being written
off by some unwise critics on the previous tour. Even
Wisden in 1980 had some harsh words: 'Gooch would
surely benefit from a more relaxed stance. His stiff, awkward position with bat unnaturally held aloft must surely
prove a severe strain when he plays a long innings in a
hot country.' In actuality, it was to prove a godsend.

4

Quickening the Pace

By 1980, Gooch was established not merely as an England batsman, but also as an England opening batsman. In 1979 he had batted in the middle order against India. Now, with Mike Brearley having given up – temporarily – Test cricket, there was no doubting that Gooch would open England's innings. That summer was his first against West Indies pace bowling. By the end of it he had scored more runs in the Test series (394) than any other batsman, and had shown he was justified by the apparent optimism of publishing his instructional book, *Batting*, before he had made a Test century.

In the course of the series he reached that first century, and it was scored, said *Wisden*, 'with an authority and power seldom seen from an Englishman in the last 15 years or so'. The test of any batsman's mettle during the 1980s was how he fared against a four-man attack of a devastation not even seen in 1976, when the West Indies still fielded medium-pacers of the likes of Vanburn Holder and Bernard Julien. If Gooch has ever been physically scared by fast bowling – and he says he has not been – he has never shown it. During the decade he had 38 innings in 19 Tests against the West Indies (itself an illustration of their strength), made 1,589 runs with four centuries and ten half-centuries at an average of 41; and this at a time when his average against Australia was in the mid-twenties. No other batsman in the world scored more runs against the West Indies in this period. It was as if he thrived when the smell of leather was strongest.

Gooch achieved all this against his growing awareness that the West Indians wore him down mentally as well as physically. 'You've really got to concentrate on every ball,' he said. 'You know that if you make one mistake against any of them it will probably be your last. Because of that, you tire more quickly.' When he faced one of them in county cricket, sometimes a lesser bowler at the other end would benefit. Cardigan Connor, for instance, has dismissed Gooch when he has survived facing Malcolm Marshall. At Test level, there was no respite. Yet, in addition to having an equable temperament, Gooch played bouncers unflinchingly. Derek Pringle, for one, is still in awe of this ability.

In 1980, Gooch had made 17 and 27 (run out) in the first Test before his century at Lord's, 123 scored out of a total of 269. His imperious driving and hooking were the features of the innings, which included a six and seventeen fours. His temperament was best shown when he attained his century without obvious apprehension, in spite of having taken twenty-three balls over the necessary last few runs. He had needed thirty-six innings to make his maiden Test century and, said Richie Benaud, who was commentating at the time, 'it couldn't have happened to a nicer fellow'. The West Indies attack was savaged in a way that it rarely has been before or since. Gooch was to bat with similar authority in the fourth Test of the series, making 83 – though he followed this with a duck in the second innings. Though he had a number of failures, there was a half-century in the final Test at the Oval that helped England stave off defeat.

In the championship he was again markedly consistent, averaging 51, against his overall first-class average of 47. He made 1,437 runs in all and again helped Essex reach the Benson & Hedges final, which they lost by six runs to Northamptonshire. Gooch made 60, the top score in his county's innings, and yet still was criticised from within his own dressing-room for his attempts to reverse sweep Peter Willey, a good friend. Gooch has continued to use the shot, if not as often or as extravagantly as Mike Gatting and company.

After two consecutive tours of Australia, Gooch was glad at the season's end to be able to stay at home – at least, until after Christmas, when England were to take on the West Indies again. For the first time he trained with West Ham, whose practice-ground at Chadwell Heath was only a few minutes' drive from his home. John Lyall, the manager, told Gooch he only had to let him know when he was coming. There were some who reckoned he had sufficient ability to play professional football, Lyall among them. For Gooch, the simple life was an idyll: football training among his own kin during the day, television supper with his wife in the evenings. He really does relish cold frosty mornings. When the time came for him to depart without Brenda for the Caribbean, he was contemplating whether the life of an international cricketer was worth it. 'My view is that no one has the right to stop me paying for my wife to fly out to join me anywhere in the world,' he wrote in *My Cricket Diary '81*. 'I can understand the argument that players are there to do a job and should be free from distraction but in my experience the comforting presence of a wife only does good to a cricketer under pressure. I would reconsider my entire future if Brenda was not allowed to join me for part of each tour.'

It was not a tour he enjoyed, for reasons other than being away from home. The political ramifications over Robin Jackman's South African connections were such that Gooch would have been quite content to return to England before the scheduled end, and most of his team-mates felt likewise. He disagreed with Ian Botham, England's captain, on a number of issues, not least running before breakfast in such a hot climate. When Botham sought the opinions of other players as to whether Gooch should desist from jogging, feeling it was tiring him out before play began, Gooch gave a withering riposte. 'You only know I jog because that's the time I always pass you on your way home from a party,' Gooch rebuked him.

Above all, Gooch's unhappiness stemmed from the death of a man who was a personal friend as much as a cricketing colleague. Ken Barrington, England's assistant manager, collapsed and died during the third Test in Barbados. Peter Roebuck, journalist and fellow opening batsman, feels that English cricket is still recovering from his death. 'Graham found in Ken genuineness and a big heart and, if he had lived, I don't believe Graham would have gone to South Africa. It was no coincidence that the team fell apart shortly afterwards.' Gooch had Brenda with him in the Holiday Inn, Barbados, when they heard. Unashamedly, they both cried. 'It was one of the saddest moments in my career,' said Gooch. 'Ken went out of his way to help players technically and was always very amenable to their wives and girlfriends. It spurred me on to be doubly determined.' The Test had to be continued and, when Gooch went in a second time, there was no mistaking for whom he was batting. His innings of 116, one of two centuries he made in the series, was achieved through going for his shots and having the capacity to forget instantaneously any playing and missing. Boycott, who was critical of this innings, put Gooch's errors down to his having grown up in the era of one-day cricket, which militated against a young batsman's technical improvement.

There were plenty of pluses. Gooch again headed both the Test and tour averages, making four centuries on the tour and 460 runs in four Tests at 57 an innings. This included 83 in Antigua and 153 in Jamaica, a thrilling attacking innings that came off only sixty-eight overs on the first day. He was notably severe on Colin Croft, having wearied of his constant short-of-a-length bowling; and many of his twenty-two fours came off Croft, mainly through cuts square of the wicket and over the slips.

Gooch's reputation now preceded him. There was no reason to suppose that he should not make runs against the 1981 Australians, and in fair measure. What happened instead was that he scored a paltry 139 runs in ten Test innings at an average of 13. Lillee was among the opposition, and for the first time Gooch encountered Terry Alderman, but neither dismissed him with regularity. Nor was he out of touch in county cricket: in nine matches he made 1,091 runs including five centuries. In the one-day internationals he performed fairly, scoring 53, 11 and 37. Such disappointing form in the Tests he attributed to a loss of confidence and muddled thinking caused by his attempts to correct his faults. But fundamentally he knew that there was nothing wrong that a big score could not put right. He did not quarrel with the selectors' decision to drop him down the order for the fourth Test. And he could not quarrel with their decision to drop him for the final Test. 'The ball moved around a lot, and two of the pitches were not really up to Test standard. Yet the truth is that for eighteen months I have had a wonderful run. No batsman gets spared lean patches and we all have to learn not to read too much into them.' So he did not alter his robust approach, knowing that his success had been built on an aggressive style, and reasoned that if he made sufficient runs in county cricket at the end of the season he would not be left out of the winter tour to India. He was told as much by the selectors. And that was exactly what happened.

Nevertheless, the fact that Gooch had been dropped fanned his inborn sense of insecurity. That year he was one of six players to sign a form indicating an interest in playing in South Africa as part of a Rest of the World eleven over a six-week period before the tour to India, for which Keith Fletcher was appointed Mike Brearley's successor. Nothing came of the proposal. Indeed, the next Gooch heard of South Africa was that John Edrich, the former England batsman, was recruiting players to go to the Republic; yet Gooch himself had not been approached. Nothing further occurred until that autumn, when Peter Cooke, the South African businessman who had originally proposed a series of matches in South Africa, came to London. Gooch and Brenda met Peter Cooke, were told that a tour was in the offing for the following March and that they would be sent a sample contract. What they were not told was that a representative South African side would be among the opposition.

So Gooch went to India in an unsettled state and as an unwilling tourist to boot. Nevertheless, had the tour been successful or merely enjoyable, Gooch most likely would not have gone to South Africa. As it was, India quickly gained a one–nil lead, and this was defended with unashamedly negative tactics and slow over rates. Gooch became in turn bored and depressed. Given the opportunity to earn what Thatcherites were beginning to call 'serious money' from a short private tour which, he felt, would not hamper his Test career, he took it.

Boycott, a friend of Cooke's and the recruiter of what became known as the South African Breweries Eleven, went home early from India through a combination of illness and dissatisfaction. Gooch envied him. That was a measure of how little he enjoyed the cricket, the dubious umpiring and the Indian food. Emburey, his great friend, felt much the same way. Yet in spite of this Gooch again made more runs in the series of six matches than any other English batsman. His 487 runs, which included a century in the fifth Test and six scores of over 40, were made at an average of 54.

Doubtless Gooch was naïve in his deliberations over going to South Africa, doubtless he was stubborn. Convincing himself that this was the right thing to do, in spite of the opinion of his wife, he treated the trip almost as if it were a crusade. He did not finally make up his mind until the end of the tour of India, having asked the organisers for certain conditions. One was that he would only go if the team was not advertised as England. The other was that he wanted more money.

'The need for security is inbred in the background of someone like Graham,' said Doug Insole (whom Gooch did not consult over going). Gooch had little money, and had been dropped by England the previous summer; and his father had recently been made redundant from John J. Dunster & Sons. Clive Radley had noticed on their first tour together how keen Gooch was to improve his lot. Insole was the one person who might have been able to persuade Gooch to stay at home, yet he discovered what was going on too late. Moreover, it was a traumatic time for him: his wife died two days before the party left furtively for Johannesburg.

When Insole telephoned Gooch's home, asked by the Test and County Cricket Board to try to persuade him 'not to be such a fool', Brenda said that Gooch had already left for the airport. 'He was beyond recall anyway,' said Insole. 'Contracts had been signed. I wrote later in his Benefit brochure that he was a bit naïve. Graham was either talked into or convinced into believing that the tour would loosen shackles on apartheid. He might look back now and say that it was a bit of a blot on the escutcheon.'

Alan Lee, then his closest journalistic friend and the co-author of *Out of the Wilderness*, Gooch's account of the trip and his subsequent ban from Test cricket, feels he regretted the loss of three years' Test cricket, and the growing introversion this caused. Gooch himself still avows that his decision was justified. 'We had had tedious draws and very slow cricket by India,' he said. 'The players were not contracted to their counties or to England, and I would always maintain it was a privately organised tour. I went for financial security and through disillusionment with Test cricket and I believe I was only carrying out my right.' That belief shone through in his own game. International cricketers rarely did justice to their talents when they toured South Africa with break-away or 'rebel' sides as they became known; Gooch was an exception.

He realised, of course, full well that the cricketing bodies around the world would not approve of what he was doing. Hence the secrecy and deception, the need to keep the planning of the tour quiet from even Keith Fletcher, his friend, mentor and captain at both national and club level. There is no ill feeling between the two over this; Fletcher himself describes Gooch as a close friend. 'I can understand that the planning had to be kept quiet, although I would not have mentioned it to anyone,' he said. 'Looking back, it would have been nice to have known earlier. I would have had more time to think about going myself.' Gooch did not wish to lead the tour party, then twelve in number, and from Johannesburg telephoned Fletcher to ask him to do so. When Fletcher declined, Gooch was saddled with the captaincy. The remainder of the players wanted him rather than Boycott, and there was scarcely anyone else who was suitable. Unwittingly, Gooch was at the eye of the storm: the side was known now not as the South African Breweries Eleven or even the Dirty Dozen but as Gooch's Eleven.

There is no mistaking the profound effect those few weeks had on Gooch's character. Especially the first week. 'I went for the money, knowing the tour would cause problems,' said John Lever. 'Graham did not think there would be repercussions. Being single-minded, he convinced himself he had done nothing wrong. It had got to him that he had been dropped by England, and there was such a difference in wages playing at county level and for England that he did not want to be merely a county cricketer since he had a family. But when he saw the press we were getting it knocked him a bit.' In England, Brenda, who had never wavered from opposing the venture, argued with her husband down a long-distance telephone line. She and the other wives and girl-friends had to fend for themselves for the first week until they, too, flew out. 'In retrospect, I should have gone with Graham,' said Brenda. 'It was the worst time. I became very confused by the whole thing. I was silly because I bought every newspaper and listened to every broadcast. We didn't have any children then, and I didn't speak to anybody. The press banged on the door and then sat in their cars waiting for me to come out, so my parents used to come round in the evening and answered any calls.' Daily newspapers were swiftly abandoned. Ten years on, the *Mail on Sunday* is the one newspaper delivered to Gooch's home. Peter Hayter, the cricket correspondent, is one of the few journalists Gooch trusts. Yet, even though he may not read many cricket reports, often as not he is all too aware of what is written about him.

Vitriolic – and supportive – letters arrived. Inevitably, he and Brenda had to change their telephone number. So, too, did Alf and Rose. 'I was upset when Graham went,' said Alf. 'We had no hard or fast views about South Africa but we were disturbed at the press he was getting. I took the *Daily Mail* then, and people were giving me reports from the *Sun* and the *Daily Mirror*. We got some flak from friends who forcibly put their viewpoint and we had one or two bad anonymous phone calls. But we didn't fall out with Graham because he was at an age when he made his own decisions and he had been in and out of the England team. I might have been naïve politically but I could not see that the players were doing much wrong. This country was still trading with South Africa and I could not understand that. The household was not upset, but it was a slightly distressing time for us.' In due course Alf visited the Republic and some of its townships and was favourably impressed. He switched to reading the *Daily Telegraph*: 'I used to think the majority of journalists were nincompoots, but I have more understanding of their job now.'

Of more concern to Gooch at the time was that Alf did not understand him. 'He believed that I had brought his name, the family name, into disrepute and that I can have no feelings for English cricket,' wrote Gooch in *Out of the Wilderness*. 'He was so upset that for a time I wondered if things between us would ever be the same again – if my mother and father would ever again come and watch me play and if they would still give advice when I asked.' It took a while to persuade both Brenda and his parents that some good might result from the whole saga. Brenda, though deeply affected, came to realise that she would see more of her husband.

Keith Pont reckoned that the press coverage Gooch received was 'a big factor in stopping him opening up to friends. A lot of people say he changed. He had always been quiet and bumbling but he laughed a great deal. As the pressures on him increased he became more of a recluse and the derogatory letters he was sent hurt him more than he showed outwardly. But he didn't take the decision half-heartedly and believes what he did was correct.' John Emburey recalls an evening with Gooch in a pub when a man persistently interrupted them. Emburey swore at him and was told by Gooch to calm down. 'In that situation Graham will just become moody and leave,' said Emburey. 'He is someone who can get depressed very quickly if things are not going well.'

Happier once Brenda had joined him in Johannesburg, Gooch took on not only the captaincy but also the task of dealing with the media, although he would not allow this to go beyond cricketing matters. Yet he found that in addition to the tour party being labelled 'Gooch's rebels' he faced resentment from those journalists who inevitably wanted to glean rather more than what he thought of Graeme Pollock's cover drive. 'When the press are seeking him out, Graham stays put in the dressing-room or retreats into his family,' said Fletcher; and, other than the formal press conferences, that was the case in

South Africa. Gooch admits that he felt victimised by the press and public, who saw him as ringleader of the tour. By the time the matches were under way, journalists had descended in droves.

Some took a harsh moral line, attacking the view that it was unfair that sport should be singled out by anti-apartheid campaigners. The point of the tour, they said, was to stage phoney Test cricket, for all Gooch's protestations that the team should not be seen as representing England. Sport had become the area in which international disapproval of apartheid was expressed. It caught people's interest and, if that was unfair, too bad. Gooch realised that his actions would be perceived as supporting apartheid and its regime yet maintained rigorously that he had no sympathy with either.

The Test and County Cricket Board were swift to react. A missive was sent by the secretary, Donald Carr, urging Gooch and the other eleven players who had signed for the tour to reconsider their positions. By the time it reached them the tour was under way and there was, anyway, no turning back. Legally binding contracts had been signed. The Board met during a match between Gooch's side and Western Province. Gooch and Brenda heard of the outcome on the World Service: a three-year ban. The news stunned him, for he had been expecting one year at most. The Board's priority, though, was to ensure that Test series against Third World nations went ahead.

Gooch reckoned they were compromising their principles over selecting sides on their merits. Just as he developed a suspicion of the media as a direct result of four weeks in the Republic, so his views on cricket administrators were coloured. An anti-establishment streak was nurtured. 'Like a lot of players he became wary of Oxbridge cliques with little power bases because he did not like the way they ran cricket,' said Emburey. Essex secretary/manager Peter Edwards (whom Gooch respects) feels that, although he and Gooch have a good working relationship, they rarely meet socially because Gooch regards him as a member of the establishment. 'He is always slightly anti-establishment yet no one has been more loyal to sponsors or the Board,' said Edwards.

Rebarbative though he had become, Gooch's mind remained uncluttered once he had a bat in his hands. Fletcher feels no cricketer absorbs pressure better. Boycott's approach to batting would have helped him in this. While others, Boycott included, struggled against high-quality South African bowling, Gooch flourished. In four first-class matches he made 396 runs, averaging 56 and winning many admirers through his powerful stroke-play. 'He was the only Englishman to do himself justice,' thundered *Wisden*. Gooch also grew to respect the tour organisers, who honoured his request, before his ban was known, to be given employment during the next two English winters. His cautious business sense was in contrast to the attitude of Emburey, who was content to sign a contract for merely the tour. South Africa's Cricket Union allowed overseas players to participate in the Currie Cup, which led to Gooch signing for Western Province.

Back in England after a tour he had genuinely enjoyed, Gooch and his fellow-players began to examine the legal implications of their ban. There were no repercussions from Essex, who appreciated that they would now have Gooch and Lever available for the whole of the 1982 season. It transpired not to be one of their more successful summers, partly because Gooch initially was out of form. The obvious reason for this would be that he was not motivated by playing merely county cricket, but he has always regarded this as too trite an explanation. Indeed, he found that he was not missing Test cricket, a residue of having not enjoyed the England tour of India. 'I worked fairly hard on him to get him into the right state of mind to play for Essex enthusiastically,' said Insole. 'He is a difficult bloke to bully but will listen to firm opinions. In the last two years of his ban, pride in Essex kept him going.' By mid-July 1982, Gooch was still short of 500 first-class runs. This in spite of an unbeaten innings of 198 against Sussex which set a Benson & Hedges record. He asked Fletcher to drop him and was talked out of it. In his next championship match he made 60 and 87; and the tide turned. He was to finish the season with 1,632 runs at an average of 44, which made him the country's leading run-maker.

When Gooch returned to South Africa that winter along with Emburey and their respective wives, there was no media interest outside of the Republic. The spot-light was on England's tour of Australia. So began two happy seasons for Gooch in Cape Town, a city of which he is especially fond. He played in the Currie Cup and various other one-day and floodlit competitions, as well as club cricket for Claremont. He had regretted not doing any coaching the previous March and opted to play once a week for an oil company, Mobil, who would include young Africans. With all this he still found he had far more spare time than during an English season. He played nine first-class matches, making 597 runs including a cen-tury off the powerful Transvaal side.

All that spoiled this idyll was a letter from Alf. In it he enclosed an 'exclusive' story from the *Sun* claiming Gooch had told their reporter, Ian Todd, that he didn't care about England any more. Gooch was furious, for the quotes were a fabrication. He was particularly incensed at the anguish caused to his father. What had happened was that Todd had been asked by his office to contact Gooch in the hope that he would say he was missing playing for England, who were not faring well in Australia. Unable to contact Gooch, Todd was informed by a South African journalist that Gooch had said he did not care about what happened to England. 'The story was based on material sent by this journalist,' said Todd. 'He told us this was what Graham had said in a different context on a previous occasion. I had to take responsibility because the story appeared under my name.' The article carried the banner headline 'I Couldn't Care Less about England'. When the case came before the High Court in 1984, Todd was not called to give evidence. The *Sun* sought not to prove the truth of what they wrote but that it did not bear the meaning that Gooch felt it did. The judge, Mr Justice Comyn, told the jury in his summing-up that they might find it 'wholly unreasonable and monstrous' to invent such an interview, which Gooch said horrified him and made him out to be disloyal, selfish and contemptibly smug. The jury awarded Gooch £25,000, which, he felt, vindicated his reputation. 'I have always wanted to play for England and if selected in the future will only be too happy to do my best for my country,' he said.

His relationship with the media had reached its nadir. Gooch would have nothing to do with Todd other than at formal press conferences, when Todd always made a point of asking him a question. In return Gooch never shirked from replying and always made a point of calling him 'Mr Todd'. 'Graham had said that if he received any criticism that was below the belt he couldn't be expected to have a beer with me the next day,' said Todd. 'I always tried to be totally professional in our working relationship, which improved only when we got to St Kitts on the 1990 West Indies tour and had a run together. We had a couple more runs after that.'

Derek Pringle feels that Gooch's dislike of press criticism stems from their attitude over his visits to South Africa. 'Graham sees it as sick that reporters can write intrusive and inaccurate things to sell papers and make a living while he himself is criticised for making his living in South Africa. He is a principled person keen to take newspapers to court because he feels they should not get away with inaccuracies.' Essentially he is upset by personal criticism, yet he has been known to storm into the press-box at Chelmsford and upbraid a reporter for wrongly describing the technical manner of his dismissal. An intolerance of reporters who were not well briefed plus a reluctance to give more than a trite answer to a trite question meant that he was better off remaining in the sanctity of the dressing-room. John Lever felt he was becoming paranoid about the press. The handful of journalists he has taken into his confidence – Lee, Hayter and David Norrie of the *News of the World*, who has become a confidant – have been left in no doubt as to what will happen to the friendship if Gooch's trust is broken.

In South Africa and, indeed, while he was playing county cricket during his ban, Gooch was mostly left alone by the media. For one thing, there were considerably fewer first-class matches in the Currie Cup and consequently considerably fewer reports. Gooch's third summer in the Republic was his most successful: 615 runs in seven matches at an average of 51 an innings, including 171 against Eastern Province. Western Province reached the finals of both the Currie Cup and the Nissan Shield, losing both to Transvaal. He was invited to speak at the opening of the pavilion at Langa, the club run by John

Passmore for Blacks in the Cape. He met no hostility within the country over playing there as a mercenary and, indeed, would have gladly continued for a third season with Western Province had he not been offered a Benefit by Essex for 1985, his first year after his ban ended. Significantly, he did not rule out returning to play in South Africa.

5

England Exile

That county cricket has never been a grind to Gooch was evidenced not only by his remarkable form for Essex after he had become England captain but also during his enforced absence from Test cricket. In 1983, the second year of his ban, he did much to help Essex win the championship for the second time in five years, making 1,227 runs including three centuries at a time they were most needed, the last month of the season. He scored heavily in one-day cricket, setting another individual record through making 176 against Glamorgan in the John Player League. The following summer Gooch won just about every award going for batting. It was his best season to date in county cricket, one in which he made 2,281 championship runs at 69 an innings and became the first player for eight years to score 2,500 first-class runs. This set an Essex record. His century against the West Indies, the first to be scored against them in a season in which they won all five Tests, gave him much pleasure. He himself felt there was no special reason for this burst of form, for his game was no different from what it had been the previous year. As England were thrashed match after match, there was a clamour for him to return; by now, though, he was too accustomed to the Test and County Cricket Board's way of thinking to feel there was the slightest chance of resuming his Test career before 1985. Playing in a highly successful team can only have helped him weather the ban: Essex won the championship again, in addition to the Sunday League.

Gooch, who turned thirty-one during the 1984 season, was now at his peak as a pitiless destroyer of bowling. Later he would become a more consistent 'percentage player', choosing to play only those shots entailing minimum risk. Emburey recalls an innings he played against Middlesex that was remarkable for its brute power. Essex needed 210 in thirty-three overs, a task Fletcher thought was out of the question. Gooch, though, was determined to have a go, and effectively he won the match. He was unbeaten on 120 when Essex gained a crucial victory by four wickets. In particular, he showed that his time spent practising with Emburey in the nets in South Africa had been put to good effect. 'We lived on each other's doorsteps in Cape Town and I used to enjoy bowling at Graham,' said Emburey. 'Unfortunately during those winters he worked out a way to play me to the extent that bowling at him in the middle became a daunting task. He played me off the back foot so that I had to pitch the ball further up, whereupon he would drive me off the front foot and sometimes hit me over the top.' Clive Radley recalls Emburey 'throwing in the towel' when Gooch, having exhausted his text-book shots, reverse-swept him.

Essex and Gooch were now commensurately successful: it was the ideal time for him to hold a Benefit. He would, almost certainly, return to play for England, whose cricket team was performing in inverse proportion to the nation's economy. The City of London directly adjoins Essex; and in these Thatcher boom years no one was doing better than Essex Man, the phenomenon coined by the journalist Simon Heffer as a direct result of commuting to Liverpool Street every day on the Chelmsford line. 'The people I shared carriages with were hard working, highly motivated by money, self-reliant and they enjoyed their leisure and lifestyle. Many of them could have been Graham Gooch if it was not for the fact that their behaviour was gross,' he said.

Those whose lifestyle included watching Essex were at least generous with their new-found wealth when the collection-buckets were passed around the ground. They appreciated Gooch's personal appearances at Benefit functions in addition to his cricket. Essex provided facilities regardless of who their Beneficiary was, and for Gooch there were numerous functions besides. Ron Cundale, chairman of Gooch's Benefit committee, who had given him some work at his shipping company at Buckhurst Hill in 1976, said: 'Normally 350 turn up for the London dinner we stage for the Essex Beneficiary. For Graham we had to put on two separate dinners for 1,224 guests.' Insole felt that Gooch put a 'tremendous effort' into ensuring his Benefit worked. 'His attitude was: "I've thrown myself into my profession, and it may or may well not go right, but I must provide for my family." He was not keen on socialising until he ran his Benefit and he ran it superbly. As chairman of Essex I received lots of messages from people who appreciated the time he had spent with them. He was pushed into a new social environment.' Cundale had been involved with organising Benefits for Essex players for the previous six years and had helped Fletcher make £82,000 from his testimonial. 'But the difference with Graham was the fantastic support he got from the big firms in the City. He was also out every night of the week collecting from the county pubs, who wanted to show their appreciation.'

Gooch's recall by England and still more Essex success –
they won the John Player League, NatWest Trophy and
reached the final of the Benson & Hedges Cup in 1985 –
only helped. Gooch netted a staggering £153,906, almost
double what Fletcher received in 1984, the year he lost
the England captaincy, and more than Geoffrey Boycott's
record sum of £147,954 the previous year. Fearing for
the future of the average county player, the Cricketers'
Association warned that the Inland Revenue might make
Benefits taxable as a result. And yet, taking inflation into
account, there was little disparity between Gooch's
Benefit earnings and what the likes of Cyril Washbrook
had made three decades before.

He was now a relatively wealthy man. Most of his
Benefit money went into a new property in Hutton, in
style, if not in distance a long way indeed from his roots.
Gooch had seen out his ban without complaint and without taking legal action over its severity, although this he
had considered. He found that the Test and County
Cricket Board had prepared themselves for this eventual-
ity and knew their ground better than they had done
during their court case with Kerry Packer. Their standpoint was that international cricket had been put in jeop-
ardy by cricketers who went to South Africa and then
expected to play in representative matches against Third
World countries. To challenge that in a court of law
would have been an expensive folly.

Any remaining doubts as to whether he would regain
his Test place against Australia in the summer of 1985
were dispelled by his form against them in the one-day
internationals. His scores were 57, 115 and an unbeaten
117, which gained him the award of England's Man of
the Series. This was far from the strongest of Australian
sides, as was proved when they lost the Ashes, but they

did possess in Geoff Lawson, Craig McDermott and Jeff Thomson three of the quickest bowlers outside the Caribbean. In a six-Test series Gooch did not play a major innings until the third Test, when he scored 70 and 48. This was followed by 74 in the fourth Test and a magnificent 196 in the final match at the Oval, which England won by an innings and plenty. Gooch batted chancelessly for 423 minutes, hitting twenty-seven fours; and his partnership with his captain, David Gower, realised 351 for the second wicket. In this, one of their rare substantial partnerships, they complemented one another much as Gooch benefited from the languid strokeplay of Ken McEwan when playing for Essex. Off the field their relationship, said Gower, was based on mutual respect. 'All cricketers tend to start a friendship by respecting each other's ability, and Graham had plenty. We got on well from the word go. What changed with him was that he became more professional and gained more pride in his performance as he grew older. He became more demonstrative in his expectations of others.' This was in pointed contrast to Gower himself, who with time seemed increasingly comatose.

For the second year running Gooch scored more than 2,000 first-class runs – 2,208 at an average of 71. For Essex, he played in just eleven championship matches owing to England appearances and yet still managed to make 1,368 runs at 91. Essex again won the John Player League and gained their seventh title in as many years by beating Nottinghamshire in the final of the NatWest Trophy. In this, Gooch made 91, putting on 202 for the first wicket with Brian Hardie. At the season's end Fletcher relinquished the captaincy of Essex, reasoning that the county would best be served if he did so at a stage when he could continue to play and thus assist the new captain tactically. There was no doubting that this would be Gooch: he was the player Fletcher had come to consult more than any other, and his status and resolve were such that he would not be overlooked. In addition, he had little competition.

His form in the final weeks of the season was unaffected by developments off it, of which, unwittingly, he was at the epicentre. Indeed, his final six first-class innings of the season realised 728 runs. Towards the end of the summer he had been asked in a radio interview whether he would visit South Africa again if the circumstances were similar. He implied that he would, exercising the right of any individual to keep an open mind about his future while having no immediate thoughts of returning there. He had written much the same in his book.

His words, though, were seized upon in the Caribbean as a threat to the stability of England's forthcoming tour of the West Indies, which was not due to start until the following January. There was all too much time for bickering. Gooch's attempts to clarify his comments and reiterate his opposition to apartheid fell on stony ground. Lester Bird, the Antiguan Foreign Minister, stated: 'We would categorically say that Mr Gooch will not be welcome in Antigua. The attempted apology falls short of what is required, I think, for Caribbean people to accept that he should come and visit this country.' Antigua was a scheduled venue for one of the Tests.

The Test and County Cricket Board at first maintained a diplomatic silence before issuing a statement on Gooch's behalf in a more apologetic tone than he would have liked. Privately, he still felt he – and every other cricketer – had the right to tour South Africa, though he condemned its apartheid. 'I thought', he said later, 'that once I had served my sentence everything would be equal.

That was one of the biggest mistakes I ever made.' Naïve
he may have been, but he took offence at Bird's self-
imposed role and was not immediately mollified when
Bird wrote a 2,000-word open letter to *The Times* which
appeared to hold out an olive branch. Gooch decided
to wait before accepting the invitation to join the tour
party. It was perhaps no coincidence that he finished
seventh and last in a Silk Cut challenge single-wicket
competition at Arundel in the last of the summer's
cricket.

Gooch talked matters over with his family. But ultimately it was the TCCB chairman Raman Subba Row
who persuaded him, perhaps against his better judgement, to join the party, which was to be captained by
Gower. It was an unqualified mistake, although, had he
not gone, he might well never have toured with England
again. In nearly all respects the trip was a disaster, and
Gooch suffered more than anyone. The very start was a
foretaste: he was greeted with placards, demonstrations
and a burning effigy of himself in Trinidad, while a real
South African, Allan Lamb, walked the streets without
so much as a murmur of disapproval.

Gooch, a reluctant tourist from the outset, became
deeply depressed. Just as he finds it hard to conceal his
feelings over sloppy cricket on the field, so any unhappiness he suffers off it manifests itself to others. Lester Bird,
even if he was also styled Deputy Prime Minister of
Antigua, was one critic; Michael Manley, former Prime
Minister of Jamaica and a more prominent figure
throughout the Caribbean, was another. He wrote of his
'lingering indignation about Gooch' and raised again the
issue of the radio interview. Then there was the leader in
the *Trinidad Express* which began: 'Go jump in a lake,
Gooch.' The article continued about Gooch 'and his fel-

low Judases who claimed their pieces of silver off the backs of the South African Blacks'.

Gooch took offence and, until Brenda came out, either retreated into himself or took refuge in the company of Emburey. He stayed clear of the news reporters who knew little of cricket but paid gleeful attention to what the likes of Ian Botham were up to off the field. Unsurprisingly, he failed to appreciate Frances Edmonds's highly successful book, *Another Bloody Tour*, feeling that her criticisms of her husband, Phil, were merely to disguise the fact that some of her information came from him. Gooch resented him for that, too. 'Graham was socially stratified (*sic*) and not easy to get on with,' said Frances Edmonds. 'But, then, the other players would also talk bullshit most of the time if we went out to dinner. He was shy and I don't understand shy people, and he made it obvious that the tour was a trial he did not have to put up with. But I had a lot of respect for his good cricket brain. He told the truth in a low-key way.'

Bob Willis, England's assistant manager on that tour, was highly critical of him. In retrospect he felt Gooch should not have gone. 'It was not difficult to see the sort of reception he would get.' In that he averaged only 27 and made a highest score of 53 (though, curiously, he had three other scores of 50 or over) in the five-Test series, his batting was undoubtedly affected, although some of the pitches were below the requisite standard and he was playing in a demoralised side. And yet he did much to quieten the demonstrators in Trinidad in the best way possible – by making England's one century on the tour in the second of the representative one-day matches. His unbeaten 129 came off thirty-seven overs and was widely acclaimed as a magnificent, regal innings. This followed the one match of his career in which he felt in danger of being hit, the first Test at Sabina Park, where the pitch was fast and uneven; yet his first-innings 51 was exemplary for the way in which he played the rising short-of-a-length ball.

After the third Test in Barbados, in which Gooch made his highest score of the series (53), before being out to a near-unplayable ball, he did not feel it worth continuing – at least, not to the very end of the tour, which would be in Antigua. Neither Peter May, the chairman of selectors, nor the British High Commissioner of Barbados, Antigua and Barbuda, was able to persuade him that he would be far better off focusing on his game and in particular on the West Indians' formidable fast bowling. May returned to London carrying a letter from Gooch to the Test and County Cricket Board, whose concern was such that Donald Carr, their secretary, was promptly dispatched to Trinidad, to where the tour party had moved for the fourth one-day international. After a meeting with Gooch, Gower and manager Tony Brown that lasted for much of the day, Carr succeeded in persuading Gooch to stay, although, it transpired, this had more to do with a personal plea from Gower. The captain, by appealing to Gooch's loyalty, talked him out of a move that could have damaged his career. Not all the players felt he should have continued, but Gower's counsel proved wise and, indeed, beneficial to England, for although England were soundly beaten through Viv Richards making the fastest Test century in terms of balls received, Gooch made two hard-earned scores of 51. The demonstrators had dwindled in numbers, yet he had shown once again his capacity for absorbing pressure. The criticism that he received now was as often as not from the English press, who felt his stance had been counter-productive. Of

Antigua's Deputy Prime Minister, no more was heard.

A tour to the West Indies, ending in mid-April, leaves scant time for respite before the next English season. For Gooch, there was all too little preparation for his first tilt at captaining Essex. In that he had seen the tour through, his Test career would inevitably continue; and that, of course, would mean missing a fair amount of county cricket. He led Essex in thirteen out of twenty-four championship matches and hence leant heavily on Fletcher to captain in his absence as well as give him tactical support. So well did they combine that Essex again won the championship, in spite of Gloucestershire having a 54-point lead at one stage. At his own admission, Gooch was no dictator; and he was quick to acknowledge Fletcher's expertise. 'I enjoyed the extra responsibility that went with captaining, but really nothing had changed. Keith is the best captain I played under, so it was marvellous to have him on the field offering advice. We did not have team-talks before a match but discussed the game all the time – Keith gave me tips about positioning fielders and sometimes moved a fielder himself. Captains do not keep books but he would log in his memory batsmen's strengths and weaknesses. All the players chipped in with suggestions,' said Gooch.

Essex had come to draw on a pool of fifteen players, what with Test calls and injuries. And they had the rare luxury of five different captains in less than a month – Gooch, Fletcher, Hardie, Acfield and Lever. Shrewdly, they signed Allan Border, Australia's captain, and John Childs, Gloucestershire's left-arm spinner. One topped their batting averages, the other took eighty-five wickets and headed their bowling. Their youth policy, in which they took particular pride, was proving notably successful. Off the field, their marketing strategies were enabling them to maintain a large staff. There was no reason, it seemed, for them not to continue their remarkable achievements, as had Liverpool in another sport.

That is not to say Gooch became a successful leader overnight. Fletcher, as with any other county captain, took several months if not years to grow into the job, albeit with a weaker staff than Gooch had in his first season. Significantly, Border felt that Gooch had it in him to become 'a very good captain'. He wrote after the season that Gooch had learned from Fletcher. 'Graham appreciated the value of Keith's style of leadership in taking guys aside for a quiet word as soon as there are any dramas. When he goes through periods of depression like we all do if we're not playing particularly well, he tends to get caught up in his own game a little bit. And then [you] forget about your captaincy duties. Maybe that happened a couple of times but he will learn from it.' Gooch has never been one to shout at players, and neither will he ever be vociferous in his encouragement, in the manner of, say, Mike Gatting. Yet everyone knows where they stand. His face is too honest to mask his feelings. Television producers have become aware of this and, when he led England in Australia four years later, the cameras would home in if a bad ball from one of his bowlers went to the boundary. The captain invariably wore a hangdog look.

Standing in the slips he will say, from time to time: 'I wish someone would bowl me a few half-volleys like that.' To him, discipline is paramount for a bowler. Neil Foster will have a go at him, telling him to stop shaking his head and that the bowlers are trying. Fletcher would say to him: 'For God's sake let the bowlers bowl.' John Lever was aware of Gooch's reactions when he bowled a bad ball: 'It is very hard not to look at the captain.'

David Acfield felt that in his initial period as Essex captain Gooch did not give his spinners sufficient credit. 'He was brought up in the era of West Indian quicks, and his top cricket has been played on flat and green pitches. Once he had decided on a plan of action he was very difficult to change. I would become important again once we got on a turning wicket.' In spite of the success Essex had in 1986, some of their players inevitably took a while to come to terms with the transition in the captaincy. Gooch's achievements surprised Keith Pont. 'Graham took such a weight on his shoulders that he never allowed us the responsibilities we had had under Keith, who put the onus on the players. Graham was intent on doing more than his share.' His natural inclination towards seamers was reinforced by Fletcher, who would play two spinners only when the pitch was likely to take turn.

Traditionally, the Essex captain has had a fair amount of power. There is no selection committee: he alone picks the team. Not unnaturally, Gooch took a while to sort out exactly who he wanted to play for him: he was prepared to wait for the end of the careers of one or two of the older players who were not so keen on physical training as he was. In turn they felt he was taking the attitude that to enjoy yourself on the field was a sign of weakness. The comedians were being replaced by the assiduous practitioners who rarely left the nets.

In his first season of captaincy, 1986, Gooch did not score the weight of runs that he and Essex had become accustomed to him making. Border put this down not to the pressures of captaincy but to a residue of his problems in the West Indies. He made 778 championship runs and 1,221 in all first-class cricket. For once, he was well down the national batting averages. Two of his three centuries were made in the Test series against India and New

Zealand; the first coming at Lord's in a match England lost. Indeed, they were thoroughly outplayed by India over the three matches, in which Kapil Dev took Gooch's wicket on four out of six occasions. Against New Zealand, Gooch again made a century at Lord's, the seventh of his Test career and one of his most important. England were dependent on him to make a large score if they were to draw a match in which Hadlee had been rampant, and he did not let them down. He batted for more than seven hours, in the latter stages with great freedom, and in compiling 183 enabled England to declare. He did not make a score of note in the last two matches of yet another losing series for England, during which touring again became an issue.

In the second New Zealand Test he was under pressure to announce his availability or otherwise to tour Australia that winter. A few days later he declined to go, although he said he would be available for the one-day matches after Christmas in the event of injury. He had not enjoyed his last England tour – a bloody tour indeed – nor, for that matter, the two before that; yet there was another factor that influenced his decision. 'When one has done five or six tours it depends on individual circumstances whether one wants to go again,' he said. Those circumstances were his twin daughters, Sally and Megan. Gooch was simply loath to leave such a young family for four months. He also saw himself as a modern father, prepared to go to bed at nine in the evening if the young nanny was away and it was his turn to do the feeding in the small hours. 'Our three children put me under pressure,' he said at the time. 'I have become conditioned to losing sleep and not being able to read the papers during the day. If we had not had twins, I might have gone to Australia. Yet I am enjoying being a father.'

He had looked into the possibility of taking a flat in one of his favourite cities, Sydney, where the family could be based, but this was not feasible. The itinerary and the number of flights England had to undertake precluded it. They would not in fact have played their first day's cricket in Sydney until 15 January, more than three months after arriving in Australia. Emburey telephoned Gooch to tell him the travelling was horrendous: there was no time off. Sooner or later certain players were bound to react to the incessant cricket and travelling that England were being asked to undertake, and Gooch, of course, was fortunate in that he could afford not to tour. He received his fair share of criticism, some of which he did not find fair at all: he did not think much of one correspondent's incredulity that he could put Brentwood before Bondi. What he would have liked to do was to return to South Africa – not to play there (he had been sounded out) but to visit Ken McEwan, who had retired from county cricket and with whom he kept in touch through cassette tapes sent through the post. If he did, he knew he would 'get it in the neck', as he put it.

He did not idle the winter away. England had no need of him in Australia, but he joined them for a limited-overs tournament in Sharjah that lasted twelve days (where he first worked with and impressed Mickey Stewart, the England manager). He trained three days a week with West Ham, shovelled topsoil in his garden, lost weight through running and spent four days in Hong Kong contesting another all-rounders challenge. Then in January he began a new job which made him think he might not tour again: he had left Duncan Fearnley, the batmaker, to whose firm he had been contracted since 1979, to promote equipment and clothing for Stuart Surridge, the cricket manufacturer. He would also undertake public relations work for them.

Gooch had known Stuart Surridge's son, 'Tiger', one of the directors, for ten years. They were friends: 'Tiger' Surridge regarded him as a friend for life, and the deal offered to Gooch was not merely more lucrative than his contract with Fearnley. There was a tacit understanding that he could join Stuart Surridge when he retired from playing, an attractive arrangement not least because their factory was twenty minutes' drive from Gooch's home. The firm had not had a top-class cricketer on their books since Viv Richards left them in 1980 and were keen to modernise their image.

The liaison turned out to be a markedly happy one. 'Graham has given us better value than we would have reckoned at the outset, and in return gets as good a deal as any cricketer,' said 'Tiger' Surridge. 'He has been the best of all our players to deal with. He never lets a retailer down – he turns up early, signs bats, does some coaching and always writes a thank-you letter for having him. He is more intelligent than people would credit him and has a flair for designing products. It was his idea to produce bats called "Turbo Test Selection". He signs each one personally, and we sell six hundred a year. He has designed tracksuits, gloves and pads for us, and when we introduced a pouch rather than a jock-strap to hold a protective box he came up with the name "Box Briefs". We sold thousands and thousands. He will go through bats at the factory to sort out which feel good. And, as a result of him joining us, so, too, did other Essex players.' Gooch also set up exhibitions, some of which continued during the summer. He was able, now, to laugh when he was asked if he would revert to toolmaking after his playing days were over. Apart from anything else, his qualification was as good as useless with the advent of computerised machinery and metrication.

The winter's break had renewed his zest for the game, and there was no reason to suppose that he should not win back his England place. What happened instead was that he ran into the worst form of his career. Having begun with 55 against MCC and batted in imperious style in making 171 off 206 balls against Gloucestershire, he recorded pairs in his first four innings at Chelmsford, against Warwickshire and the Pakistanis. He seriously wondered if he had lost his ability for good. 'I can't play any more,' he told Emburey, who tried to reassure his friend in the same way that Gooch had reassured him when he had had difficulties with his bowling. Without Border in the middle order, and with Paul Prichard having shattered a finger in April, Gooch felt the Essex batting would collapse if he was out early in the innings. This may have accounted for the way he was performing, falling over to the off side, playing too much to leg.

'I found myself wondering if I had lost it for good,' he said. 'As a professional sportsman you must worry when it goes seriously wrong: it affects your enjoyment, you start to wonder whether the mental pressure is all worth it. You need that enthusiasm that makes you want to get out there and do it. I was wondering if it had all caught up with me. Obviously I felt I could still do the things I could ten years earlier, but I started to notice that I felt exhausted after a hard day's play. I was slowing up and feeling less sharp.' He felt that the only way to sort himself out was to go back to basics. His loss of confidence was compounded by his cares over the captaincy, that he had insufficient time to prepare for an innings. It was difficult enough to follow Fletcher, and he was always mindful of what others were thinking. 'There are so many things coming into my head that a bowler could bowl me a half-volley and I would not notice it,' Gooch would tell colleagues. Moving house did not help, either, and having twin daughters invariably meant that his sleep was disturbed. 'Getting the kids to sleep was a terrible job,' said Brenda. 'The twins climbed into our bed at night. There are times when I woke up in the morning and didn't know who was there.'

Gooch's form did improve in the second half of the summer to the extent that he made 1,100 championship runs at an average of nearly 40 and headed the Essex averages. He took to batting in the middle of the order. Earlier in the season England's selectors chose him to bat at number three for the first one-day international against Pakistan, in which he made 9. They did not choose him again that summer. When he was selected for MCC's Bicentenary match in August, this was only because Martin Crowe, the New Zealand batsman, dropped out.

On the eve of the match, Gooch discussed the Essex captaincy with Doug Insole. By their own high standards the county were having a poor season and were unlikely to win anything. 'Graham asked me if I thought he would be letting anyone down by giving up as captain,' said Insole. 'He asked me whether he would be able to have another go if he did give up.' Reassured by his chairman and with his mind unencumbered, Gooch rediscovered his form and confidence the very next day. Batting first wicket down for MCC against the Rest of the World, he made an authoritative 117 from 210 balls, an innings that gave him such satisfaction he could even smile in admiration when Roger Harper ran him out with a brilliant pick-up and throw. Gone were his technical faults. Upright and still at the crease, he removed Abdul Qadir from the attack, an achievement few, if any, of his England colleagues had managed in preceding Test series against Pakistan. Gooch had a wry attitude towards batting against Qadir's leg spin: 'Reading him is one thing, playing him is another.' His form continued in the second innings, in which he made 70 in 118 balls.

In addition to consulting Insole over the Essex captaincy, Gooch also confided in Fletcher. He did not discuss it with any of his other colleagues, which upset John Lever and Alan Lilley. 'I had never seen anybody of his ability constantly being out for ducks. We might have been too critical of him, especially since Keith Fletcher didn't become a great captain overnight. But I was hurt he did not consult me before he gave up. If there is a criticism to be made of him, it is that he should consult more often,' said Lever. Lilley, who had been given his county cap by Gooch, learned of his decision on television and was similarly dismayed. They had become close friends on account of training and driving together: among Lilley's nicknames was 'Andy', after Ian Botham's former driver, for Gooch would rather sleep than take the wheel. Six years Gooch's junior, Lilley had also learned his cricket playing for Ilford. 'A gut feeling keeps them together,' said Derek Pringle. 'Their friendship is based on honesty and not crossing each other.' Gooch is aware that Lilley, perhaps more than any other cricketer, could sell details of his home life to national newspapers. He is equally aware that Lilley never would.

Their friendship has grown stronger since Lilley retired. He had never been assured of a place in the side, was left out by Gooch, and his opportunities were especially limited during Gooch's ban from Test cricket. 'Graham didn't captain the side badly, but he was very selfish at first. When he came off the field after being out he would go running. As a young player, I thought he should be in the dressing-room,' said Lilley. 'I remember him getting annoyed with me at the ways I was out – he expected me to be as good as him, and I had to tell him I wasn't. But it was very hard for him to lead the side with Keith Fletcher still playing.'

Gooch maintains that others might have been affected by his intentions. 'I did not want my batting worries to rub off on the rest of the lads. The captaincy on the field was not a problem . . . It was the bits and pieces away from the middle that meant I was not giving a hundred per cent either to the captaincy or my batting. There wasn't time for me to concentrate on what I wanted to do best for the team – at ten-forty I like to be changed, everything ready, padded up, gear on and just sit there calm and placid and silent and put into my mind those thoughts about concentrating on the positive, drumming out the negative. I suppose it will always be held against me that I packed in the job because my absorption with batting affected my captaincy.' Essex were fortunate in that Fletcher was willing to assume the role once more, although it transpired that he left himself out of their side for half the following season, reasoning that if he played, Nasser Hussain, their promising young batsman, would not be given the opportunities he deserved. Ironically, Gooch was to find himself captaining both club and country by the end of the season – and, having recovered his form, he found neither to be a burden.

His batting in the World Cup in the autumn of 1987 had much to do with this. He made one or two technical adjustments and found that some good pitches in Pakistan and India gave him confidence. This is a tournament he has always relished. He began soundly with 47 and a disciplined innings of 92 against the West Indies, 21 and 16 off Pakistan, 84 and 61 against Sri Lanka. In no small way did his runs help England reach the semi-finals. They were to play India, and resolved that the two spinners, Shastri and Maninder Singh, should not be allowed to bowl their overs cheaply. 'Graham was desperately keen to win the World Cup,' said Mike Gatting, then England's captain. 'He worked out how he was going to play the spinners and spent two days before the semi-finals in the nets. At the end, a little boy who bowled at him said: "Mr Gooch, have I bowled that badly that you swept every ball?" It was for a purpose, and he proceeded to play very well.'

Gooch scored 115 off 136 balls with eleven fours, and with Gatting swept and pulled Shastri and Maninder Singh repeatedly. They enabled England to reach the final against Australia. In this, Gooch made 35 and took a wicket in eight overs at a cost of 42 runs. England did not win, Gatting taking the blame for their defeat on account of the notorious reverse sweep through which he lost his wicket. No country batting second has made as many as 254 to win in the tournament; at 135 for two England had an excellent chance to do so. But Gatting contrived his own demise in Allan Border's first over.

Gooch had informed England's selectors he would be available for the subsequent tour of Pakistan, which would continue until Christmas, but not for the visit to New Zealand beginning in January. He had enjoyed the World Cup and felt it was well organised. Also, there had been no objections or demonstrations over what was now familiarly termed his 'South African connections'. Yet England's visit to Pakistan was ill-conceived and turned out to be another unhappy tour.

It was almost abandoned after the infamous row on the field between Gatting and Shakoor Rana, the umpire. Certainly Gooch would not have allowed himself to be provoked to the extent of wagging a finger in an official's face; yet as a batsman he was all too aware of the standard of umpiring. 'We were ready to pack our bags after the Shakoor Rana incident,' said Gatting, 'and Graham was very supportive throughout. He was very positive, a professional trying to do a professional job. He went about his job quietly and always came up with advice when I asked for it.' In the three one-day internationals, all won by England, Gooch made 43, 142 with fourteen fours off 134 balls, the second-highest score by an England player in this form of the game, and 57. There was little inkling of the problems to come.

In the first Test at Lahore, Gooch made 12 and had reached 15 in the second innings when he was given out, caught at slip off Iqbal Qasim. Gatting was at the other end. 'Graham's bat missed the ball by two inches. He looked at me as if to say, "What are we doing here?" It was just one of many bad decisions but we thought after that we had better get a bat on the ball.' Gatting complained about the umpiring after the match, which Pakistan won by an innings with a day to spare. The match will best be remembered for one particular incident, the second-innings dismissal of Chris Broad, who was given out, caught at the wicket, also off Iqbal Qasim. Almost a minute had elapsed before he departed. Had Gooch not been at the other end and ushered him off, he might still be there today.

Lahore was followed by Gatting's altercation with officialdom at Faisalabad, where Gooch made 28 and then 65 from 74 balls in the second innings as England strove in vain to make up for the loss of an entire day's play that was given over to wrangling. In the third Test, played on a flat pitch at Karachi, Gooch foreshadowed future match-saving efforts with a dogged 93 in 375 minutes in

England's second innings, which ensured Pakistan would not win. A tasteless series was called off in the tea interval. Gooch was not alone in his delight at returning to Christmas in England. For him at least, there was to be no further cricket that winter.

6

A Late Call

At the end of England's tour of Pakistan, Gooch made his intentions public. 'I can't see me touring with England again,' he said. 'But my decision to stay at home in future doesn't mean I don't want to play for England. I just want to spend more time with Brenda and the kids. I love my cricket and touring, but I want to see them – Hannah is four and a half and the twins are eighteen months – growing up. I can't have it both ways. It's the old Catch-22 situation – whichever one I choose, the other has gone for ever. After half a dozen tours, the novelty has worn off. You're back in the hotel in Pakistan by five o'clock, which leaves you six hours to kill. That's a lot of time, every night for twelve weeks.'

He spoke his mind, too, about the umpiring in Pakistan. 'It's a joke. You learn to live with the odd mistake but there's no point playing if you're continually on the wrong end of suspect decisions. I wouldn't have minded having my stumps flattened. At least I'd have known I was definitely out. Incompetent umpiring put our livelihood at risk. A disastrous series could have cost someone his Test career.' He said he knew Mike Gatting would make an apology for the fiasco in Faisalabad. 'I've experienced the pressures he was under. When two sides can't be reconciled, one has to back down – and it's always us.

We're told: "You're right, but for the good of cricket you must make a sacrifice." Mike was used, exactly the same way I was used in the West Indies. But in Pakistan the truth came out. The dirty linen was out for all to see.'

Having resigned the Essex captaincy because he felt his form had been affected, Gooch worked – for the first time in his career, he said – at developing a positive mental approach to batting. He consciously told himself he was going to play well and score heavily. 'There was no more waiting for the worst to happen, no more negative thoughts. I forced myself to recall the times when I had done particularly well against the bowlers I was due to face that day. None of this stuff about "Oh God, it's Malcolm Marshall today – is he going to knock my off stump out of the ground for the tenth time on the trot?"' Stirring words, but he put them into action in the very first match of the 1988 season. Played over four days, it realised a record number of runs (1,570) for a county championship fixture. Essex beat Kent, the county they regarded as their arch-rivals, and in doing so Gooch made his career-best score till then, 275.

The pitch was ideal, the attack no more than average, even though Kent were to lead the championship table for much of the season. The batting was awesome. Gooch struck twenty-seven fours and four sixes, facing 399 balls. 'I got my feet moving at the right time, sorted out my pick-up and thought positively. When you are in the right frame of mind you just go out there and do it naturally,' he said. He showed, too, as he often does, that he does not lack motivation to make a second big score in the same match. Not for him the temperamental attitude of the star intent on saving his best for Test cricket. In the second innings he made 73, helping Essex to win by eight wickets.

There were further experimental four-day matches that summer. Gooch had ambivalent feelings over this, not wishing to see Essex lose their festival weeks and reckoning that three days was long enough for a decent encounter. All bowling came alike to him that sun-kissed summer: he finished the season with 2,324 first-class runs, 235 fewer than in his self-styled *annus mirabilis* of 1984, when he had eight more innings. 'I was very pleased', he said, 'at the way I came out of the lowest ebb of my career the previous year.'

For Essex he averaged 70 and reached 1,000 runs for the season in just ten innings. In only five out of twenty-one matches did he fail to make a half-century. When Fletcher unselfishly dropped out of the side to make room for Hussain, Gooch discovered that captaining was far from the burden he had found it to be the previous season: the difference now was that he was in form, outstanding form. By arriving half an hour earlier at the ground he was able to attend to the numerous chores that are a captain's lot – and have sufficient time to prepare himself for an innings. Indeed, he ended the season with such a flurry, making his sixth century in the final match against Northamptonshire, that he was keen to have a further full-time attempt at the captaincy. He had proved beyond doubt that he could shoulder such responsibility and still make runs.

There were other factors. Fletcher had decided to retire, and there was no other likely successor. Gooch realised, too, that he might have become too concerned about his own game the previous season. 'He thinks that there is more wrong with him than actually is the case,' said Lilley. Gooch was aware others felt he was becoming too critical, too meticulous. 'I have been thinking more and more about doing myself justice and was unhappy with

Balance and poise to the fore during one of Gooch's first
practice sessions *(Alf Gooch)*

A boy amongst men. Playing for East Ham Corinthians as
a twelve-year-old in 1965, wearing an Essex Schools cap.
His father is seated second from the right *(Alf Gooch)*

Alf Gooch at home in Gidea Park with one of his treasured scrap-books that have logged his son's achievements throughout a long career *(Alf Gooch)*

Early days with Essex. Batting against Leicestershire at Chalkwell Park, Leigh-on-Sea, Gooch is taken at the wicket by Roger Tolchard off the bowling of Ken Shuttleworth *(Alf Gooch)*

The cocked trigger in the era of flared trousers *(The Times)*

Leading out the breakaway England Eleven at Johannesburg after losing the toss to South Africa. Geoff Boycott, followed by Bob Woolmer, makes a rare appearance in a sun hat *(AP)*

Four England captains pictured at the Oval during 1986. From left, Ian Botham, Graham Gooch, Mike Gatting and David Gower *(S & G)*

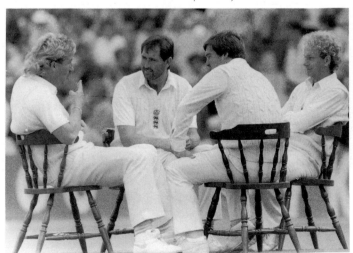

Looking for the boundary during the Benson & Hedges final against Leicestershire in 1985. Gooch made 57 *(Sunday Times)*

Overleaf Driving against Sri Lanka under the watchful eye of David Constant at Lord's in 1988 *(The Times)*

Captain of England but not of Essex: Gooch, as ever encouraged by his friend and mentor, Keith Fletcher, in his year off from leading his county *(PA)*

my technique in 1987 yet still ended up averaging nearly thirty-nine, so perhaps I got some of it out of proportion,' he admitted. Certainly he was content with the way in which he played the West Indies in the summer of 1988, a turbulent one for England. The only player to be selected for all five Tests, he made 459 runs at an average of 45.

His batting was outstanding in the first Test at Trent Bridge, when he became the sixteenth England batsman to score 4,000 Test runs. He made 73, putting on 125 for the first wicket with Broad out of a total of 245; and when Viv Richards declared, leaving England with a day and thirty-one overs to survive, Gooch ensured they did exactly that. He batted for six hours and fifty minutes in making 146 against the West Indians' customary four-man pace attack abetted by some occasional off-spin.

The first Test was the last in which Mike Gatting captained England, on account of his nightcap with a barmaid during the match. Just as the England selectors flirted with players during the series – in all, twenty-three were chosen, a disastrous policy against such a strong side – so now they toyed airily with captains. Initially, these did not include Gooch, who was, none the less, far from resentful. John Emburey was made captain for the second Test at Lord's, which the West Indies won with some ease. Gooch made 44 out of a first-innings total of 165, and in such a manner as to show that he was now the percentage player rather than the aggressor of his first series against the West Indies in 1980. He spent an hour and forty minutes in the thirties, unthinkable eight years earlier. Twice he was dismissed by Malcolm Marshall, in the second innings after making 16. Marshall was yet again the match-winner, taking ten wickets for the third time in a Test.

At Old Trafford, England were overwhelmed still more decisively, bowled out for 135 and 93. Gooch's first-innings score of 27 was one of the better efforts. Emburey was then dropped for the fourth Test and replaced by Christopher Cowdrey, whom Gooch had known since they played golf together in the Cape several years before. They got on well, even though Cowdrey was once moved to criticise Gooch over a manufactured finish to a county match. When Cowdrey, clearly nervous, was to speak to the England players on the eve of the match, Gooch pre-empted him. 'Let's get behind Chris,' he said. 'I'm fed up with losing to this lot.' It was a generous gesture but made little difference. England again lost heavily. Gooch made 9 in their first innings, once more dismissed by Marshall, but was top scorer in the second innings with 50 out of 138. Uncharacteristically, he was out chasing a wide ball, this from Courtney Walsh.

When Cowdrey withdrew from the fifth Test through a foot injury, Peter May, the chairman of selectors, had little option but to make Gooch captain: it was a simple process of elimination. Yet just as May might well have gone for a captain from outside the selected party had Cowdrey withdrawn earlier, so Mickey Stewart, the team manager, would have had Gooch as captain for the third Test. 'Emburey was the obvious choice as vice-captain. I wanted Graham because of Cowdrey's limitations as a player against a strong West Indies side. I had worked with Graham for the first time in Sharjah in 1987 and reckoned then he had leadership qualities. His public image was quite wrong. I found him to be very caring for the game and the players around him. He had tremendous pride and a belief that, once given responsibility for your county and country, you followed it through. He had similar qualities to Mike Gatting. But he thought he would be unlikely to be made captain against the West Indies because of what had happened to his batting the previous year.' Gooch was the fourth England captain of the series in his sixty-seventh Test; only four people had played more matches before leading England for the first time.

If he needed confidence, a measure came from making two decent scores, 56 and an unbeaten 67, in his previous match for Essex – against the West Indies. He won the toss and batted on a pitch of some bounce and pace, as was to be expected at the Oval after a long hot summer. He himself lasted only until the eighth over, beaten by a near-unplayable ball from Curtly Ambrose. England's middle order of Bailey, Robin Smith, Maynard, Capel and Richards – not necessarily the batsmen Gooch himself would have chosen – fell away badly. Yet the West Indians themselves collapsed, dismissed by Foster and Pringle for 183 on the hottest day of the series. England had a lead of 22: there was the prospect of Gooch bringing off a victory which would prove every bit as memorable as that by Brian Close over the West Indies at the Oval in 1966.

The latest in Gooch's procession of England opening partners was Worcestershire's Tim Curtis; and the pair began with a promising half-century opening stand. Yet when Curtis, Rob Bailey and Robin Smith were out in the space of half an hour Gooch resorted to defence – 'allying grim determination to his solid technique without ever finding his best touch or timing', as *Wisden* put it. He batted through the innings in sultry weather against bowlers who were swinging the ball and maintained a desperately slow over rate, for seven hours and eight minutes. When he was last out to Ambrose, he had batted for longer than he had ever done before without making a century. Only Foster, the nightwatchman, supported him, scoring 34. The next-highest score was Curtis's 15. Gooch had shown, as he had already when playing for Essex, that his game could be enhanced by the responsibilities of captaincy. England still lost the match – and by eight wickets, due to a century opening stand by Gordon Greenidge and Desmond Haynes; but they had regained a shred of self-respect. The flag of St George would not have to flutter at half-mast on the pavilion roof indefinitely.

The question now was whether Gooch would retain the captaincy for the one Test against Sri Lanka later that month. Logically, Cowdrey would be recalled. He had been appointed originally for two matches, built up by May as the style of leader England needed. He had recovered from injury, and his Kent side were still likely to win the championship. The selectors, though, plumped for Gooch, who was worthy of his place as a player. It was also an indication that they wanted him to lead England to India. This, although they knew by now he had agreed to join Western Province to fulfil the outstanding year of his contract that had not been taken up owing to his Benefit. For his part, having captained England for the first time, he felt a sense of pride and a desire to carry on. He had found that Stewart could take care of the peripheral tasks, and he enjoyed encouraging those players who were new to Test cricket. The selectors realised they had a captain who took his responsibilities seriously.

Needless to say, the match against Sri Lanka came as a respite to those who had grown weary of West Indian pace. England had not won for eighteen Tests: here was the ideal opportunity to do something about it. The outcome was more or less assured from the first morning when Sri Lanka, put in by Gooch, collapsed to 63 for 6. They recovered to muster 194, whereupon England's main batsmen all performed consistently. Gooch's contribution was 75. As at the Oval he batted responsibly, if seemingly over-cautiously, against a persevering but modest attack. He was in for four hours and nineteen minutes. Then, in the second innings, with his side needing only 97 to win and time not an issue, Gooch took an hour and a half over 36. There were two sessions of play remaining on the final day when England won a Test at Lord's for the first time in five years.

Gooch's leadership was regarded as just about the only heartening aspect of England's cricket during the summer. His authority as a batsman gained him the respect of colleagues and opponents alike. He was praised by the prescient editor of *Wisden*, Graeme Wright, who was almost alone in his belief in Gooch. 'He has an ability to distance himself sufficiently from his team-mates to gain their respect as a leader. He will not need to be one of the lads. I do not share the concern that his batting will suffer from his being captain. Essex consider he is capable of doing the job and they are a county who plan carefully and have a commitment to success,' he wrote in his notes for the 1989 edition. Wright could understand why the selectors wished to retain Gooch as captain, even though his intention was to spend the winter in Cape Town. Not only that. Just before the Sri Lankan Test, Gooch had admitted he was among those English cricketers who had been offered terms to take part in an international single-wicket competition in South Africa in September, lasting for two days.

Gooch's stance was that he had not signed a contract and would not be breaking any rules if he did; he would be travelling and competing as an individual rather than representing any breakaway side, and this would not breach the British interpretation of the Gleneagles Agreement. He said that, if he were to tour India, any such venture would be ruled out. In the context of international sport and politics, he could not have believed his participation would be treated as innocent or irrelevant. England's management were attempting to change his mind and persuade him to tour India, doubtless as captain. Another clandestine visit to South Africa would be a disaster, sabotaging the fragile relationships between black and white nations. If Gooch had by then agreed to captain England in India, the tour would probably be abandoned, leading to further problems for the International Cricket Conference, who were due to have another debate on South Africa the following January. Allegedly the players would earn around £8,000 each, not a great sum by South African standards.

Gooch remained adamant he would not take part, issuing his press statement, as the *Guardian* put it, 'with all the puritan monosyllables of a grim roundhead'. He was tiring of the topic being raised. 'Everyone still harks on about South Africa. I can't change what happened, can I? What's done is done. Obviously it still gets thrown back in my face all the time. I have to live with it, that's all. When we went in 1982, South Africa was a political thing, sure, but since then it's become one of the major political issues in the whole world. Certainly I feel sorry for the cricketers there of every race. They are trying desperately to do the right and honest thing by themselves and their government but I don't think there's much hope for them as things stand.'

Gooch's dilemma had not altered. If he went to India, his family could hardly accompany him, especially since his eldest daughter had started school. If he went to Western Province, his family could be with him for at least part of the time. 'I read all that stuff about not touring in the winter with England, not putting my country first, like I'm a traitor or something. It's not that I wanted to miss the cricket – I love that, especially in India, honestly – but at thirty-five I should be allowed, surely, to make a judgement between developing my career and developing my involvement with the family. What's most important? Obvious, isn't it? It's very hard not to be swayed when they say, "Daddy, Daddy, where are you going? Why are you going from us again, Daddy?" Well, I know other people think I'm wrong on that and my career comes first – or they might not be able even to consider it themselves – but, when I've weighed up everything, sometimes I've decided to put my family first. It is very hard when people start saying "Gooch sacrifices country's needs". It's my career, sure, but it's only a game as well after all, isn't it?'

Gooch told the selectors he was available to continue as captain in India, if required. Twice the selectors delayed making a decision on the captaincy, leading some to maintain he was forcing their hand. Gooch stonewalled over all such enquiries, feeling he did not consider it his business to discuss the matter. Later he was to insist that there was no question of him going to India only if he were made captain. He was, though, widely blamed for the delay in the announcement, facing accusations ranging from dithering to deviousness. The selectors' prevarication was also interpreted in this case as Gooch not being seen as a captain in the long term. The theory was that his tactics were stereotyped, his reserved public front exasperating. John Woodcock, the *Times* cricket correspondent, wrote: 'A good batsman, uneasy with the mysteries of captaincy, Gooch is being treated at the moment with the deference that might have attended a "W. G." in his heyday. It seems to me that our administrators have gone mad. Either that or I have.' E. W. Swanton wrote in the *Cricketer*: 'Among those who have seen most of him as a captain I have found no one who regards him as a natural leader, either in terms of personality or tactics. It is not disputed that the selectors extended the availability deadline for India for his convenience.' Yet Gooch had not been approached about the captaincy or his availability for touring before he signed for Western Province.

The selectors decided to appoint Gooch. That in itself was provocative, even if May did point out that their judgement was not influenced by politics and that Gooch's presence had been perfectly acceptable to the Indian Cricket Board during the World Cup the previous year. The issue became inflammatory owing to Gooch having to obtain release from his contract with Western Province in order to accept the captaincy. England were almost daring India's government to make an issue of it.

Reaction in India was predictable. The Sports Minister announced that a special meeting would be called to consider Gooch's links with South Africa. A growing band of politicians wanted a ban on all sportsmen who maintained such connections. They hinted they would continue to harass Gooch and England throughout the eleven-week tour.

There was strong reaction, too, from former England captains, notably Ted Dexter, who was critical of Gooch's captaincy, and Brian Close, who was opposed to his appointment: 'The selectors should hold their heads in shame because they have sacrificed the proud principle that the man who captains England must be prepared to serve his country in any capacity. The fact that he was contracted to a South African provincial side is neither here nor there. How can they reflect they have put in charge a guy who was only prepared to tour as skipper?' Gooch retorted by insisting he had not blackmailed the selectors.

In early September, India's Foreign Ministry announced that no player 'having or likely to have sporting contact with South Africa' would be granted a visa. It was inevitable that the tour would be cancelled since this applied to eight of the players. In one of the last county matches of the season, Gooch cocked a snook by wearing the Western Province cap. On the same day, Stewart announced that not one England player had signed his tour contract, in effect encouraging players to accept invitations to go to South Africa.

Gooch was adamant he had done nothing wrong in signing for Western Province and that, even though he had forewarned Stewart, he did not have to inform the selectors or the press of his plans. Again he made it clear that he was keeping an open mind about returning to the Republic. 'Players who go there do a lot towards helping all cricketers, yet they are picked on because they have a high profile and create a lot of publicity,' he said. 'Governments want it all ways – for their players to come here and for those who have been to South Africa not to play in their countries. I think the Cricketers' Association will be very opposed to playing with overseas cricketers in county cricket if there is a ban on English players who have been to South Africa.'

And yet, even though the tour of India had been cancelled, Gooch had no immediate plans to do anything other than spend the winter in Essex. He had taken a holiday in Portugal at the end of the season and had signed a contract with the Test and County Cricket Board. If a substitute tour was arranged, he would have no option but to go on it. This, though, did not materialise. He was paid a fair proportion of his tour fee and spent his time attempting to trim himself down to fourteen stone through training with West Ham and on futuristic gadgetry at the Barbican Health Club in London. His garage was converted into a weight-training room. He was an honorary member of Chelmsford Athletic Club (he could not become a member as he was a professional sportsman) and went cross-country running. He competed in four half-marathons. He belonged also to Thornton Park golf club and participated in a charity event organised by the Conservative Party. He made the most of his passion for tennis, at which, according to David Gower, he played a percentage game similar to his cricket. He and his family took part in a television programme on learning how to ski. Above all, he, ever the modern father, was content to bath and nappy-change the twins – and how many of his England predecessors can one imagine in *that* role?

Having found that leading England was, in some respects, an easier task than captaining Essex, Gooch was not intent on relinquishing the honour lightly. 'The captaincy came to me by accident rather than design. I had not desperately sought it out but having been given the job my views changed. I am ready to play under whoever is chosen, but that does not mean I am abdicating,' he said.

He reiterated this view as winter turned to spring and May was succeeded by Ted Dexter as chairman of selectors or, as he was styled in his salaried post, chairman of the England committee. Gooch needed to state his position since Dexter, wearing his journalistic hat, had made the most memorable remark anyone was ever likely to make about Gooch. Dexter reported on cricket for the *Sunday Mirror* (a job from which, retrospectively, Dexter felt he should have been sacked) and was required to give frank opinions. When Gooch was made captain, he did exactly that. 'If you've ever been hit in the face with a wet fish you'll know how I've been feeling this week ever since England's latest Test leader voiced his opinion on the business of captaincy,' he wrote. ' "A team is only as good as the players. Nobody can turn a bad team into a good one." That was the gist of what this amiable batsman from Essex had to say about his brief spell at the head of affairs. No wonder the England team is in such a sorry state if that is the general atmosphere in the dressing-room. How can new young players like Matthew Maynard and Rob Bailey possibly hope to play better than ever before in their lives – which is what they needed to do at Test level – if they were simply left to their own devices? A captain must make his men feel that everything is possible. The Gooch approach means that the West Indians were inevitably going to win at the Oval and that he was resigned to that result before the game began. Translate his theories on to the battlefield and there would never be a victory against the odds. David would never had killed Goliath because it wasn't worth a try. Why do I feel so miffed? Because I am being asked to believe that all my work in 30 Test matches as captain of England could just as well have been done by anyone else or by nobody at all.'

After an emotional outpouring like that, it was clear that Gooch would be unlikely to remain captain. Dexter was soon saying – in his official role – that Gooch had little leadership experience and that it was 'a very open question' as to who would captain England in the summer of 1989. 'If Graham had taken the team to India and done well, there would be no doubts. But the tour did not take place – that is why the job remains open.' On one matter, at least, they were certain to agree. Both were in favour of initiating a system of contracts for a squad of England players.

'We have been heading in this direction for some time, but now that winter employment in South Africa is out of bounds for Test players it must be to everyone's advantage to establish a settled and secure squad, contracted for one year or even more,' said Gooch. Did this mean he was going back on his long-avowed intention not to tour the West Indies again – if, indeed, he was ever to tour again at all? 'I certainly don't discount touring the West Indies next winter,' he said. 'I have got plenty of enthusiasm for the game, and if the team is being organised on more professional lines I would like to continue playing a part.'

It was always likely, though, that the new chairman would appoint a captain more in keeping with his own beliefs and, perhaps, social class. That captain was expected to be David Gower, and he was duly elected, although it transpired that Mike Gatting had been the original choice of Dexter and Stewart. The chairman of England's cricket committee, Ossie Wheatley, had used his veto to block the appointment of Gatting, who was still doing penance for events in Pakistan. This power to overrule the selection panel had been introduced at the time of Dexter's own appointment. Had it been in place a few months earlier, Gooch himself would not have been made captain for the tour of India, for political reasons.

The only contact Gooch had had with Dexter was a telephone call informing him he was not going to be retained as captain. He was disappointed not to have been interviewed by Dexter and yet did not allow this to cloud their relationship. Unlike, say, Mike Gatting, Gooch has never been fiercely attached to the England captaincy, and that has proved to be a great strength. What Dexter was not yet aware of was the influence Gooch had on those who played with him, which was rapidly becoming apparent to those close to the players.

The hierarchy at Essex had long been aware of this. Fletcher, who realised that owing to the onset of middle age he might not have been able to retain his place, had announced his retirement, and the Essex committee was prepared to let Gooch have another tilt at the captaincy – partly because there was an absence of other contenders. He had proved he could lead and still make runs. 'Graham said he had learned a lot and would like to have another dart,' said Insole, then chairman of the cricket committee as well as of the club. 'I had some doubts and would not have been so keen if he had not been keen himself. We pointed out that he should be more tolerant and encouraging. Our philosophy had always been that no one was going to blame the captain or players for losing if they were trying to win.' Fletcher felt Gooch's grasp of tactics was improving and that he had learned man-management. 'Graham had become a bit more easy-going and had realised not everybody could be treated the same. That was the biggest thing he had to learn. It was the way to get the best out of players and get feed-back, too. When he first took over from me he wasn't ready and came badly unstuck. The pressures of playing both county and Test cricket got to him. Yet I always regarded him as my natural successor because, apart from being such a fine player, he was tactically sound, too.' Lilley felt Gooch liked having players looking to him for a lead, even if that added to the pressures of captaincy.

In one sense Gooch had not changed. He was not suited to committee meetings. As captain, he was on the executive committee (which would not be the case at the majority of county clubs) and was unable, anyway, to attend more than half the meetings owing to protracted periods away from home. The same was true of meetings of the cricket committee, which Graham Saville chaired in succession to Insole. The cousins spoke on the telephone a great deal (Gooch is never far from a telephone) when not together in the captain's room at Chelmsford, which doubles as Saville's office. There was no selection committee, Essex having always given their captain a good deal of power and having never employed a cricket manager. Fletcher, as captain of the Second Eleven, also sat on the cricket committee.

'The club's committee is inclined to go along with the captain's views, although I have known them go against Graham's opinions,' said Peter Edwards. 'Graham has firm beliefs on cricket matters, has a say in which players are retained and an interest in what they are paid, but he is not interested in financial minutiae. He is sensible enough not to pontificate on a topic such as the number of seats we are going to put in a stand.' Gooch could safely leave such matters in good hands. Freed from the wrangling and internal politicking that bedevilled other county clubs, he could concentrate solely on captaincy.

7

The Second Coming

The disappointment that Gooch felt at having the England captaincy taken from him was compounded by his feeling that he had had all too little time in which to prove himself and his belief that he would never be offered it again. He felt, too, he had had a good response from his players. Other cricketers might have become depressed, with their county form or captaincy suffering. But not Gooch. He merely became a better leader. Insole was soon of the opinion that he had become a 'very good' captain and was especially taken with his encouragement of young players. Fletcher would tell an individual he was not playing but would not explain why not; Gooch now would go into detail. And he did so in a straightforward manner. Alan Lilley could accept being dropped by Fletcher but not by Gooch, one of his closest friends; he disagreed when Gooch told him Hussain, who had made his début only the previous season, was the better player, but subsequently came to realise that this was in the best interests of the club. 'Graham handled his dropping of me in a professional way. He treated me no differently to anyone else, which stopped other players from thinking I was going to be treated favourably because of our friendship.' Saville reckoned that Gooch had an 'awful job' dropping Lilley. Once Lilley was out of the side and subsequently appointed Essex Youth Development Officer, their friendship burgeoned to an even greater extent. Lilley, who still trains with Gooch and regards him as the most dedicated person with whom he played, made him his best man when he remarried in 1991.

Gooch's preference for the younger player here was characteristic. 'I have never had to say to Graham: "Isn't it about time you gave so-and-so a go?"' said Insole. Given the choice between an established player and a promising but unproven younger man, Fletcher would generally plump for experience. Gooch, though, was willing to take a chance. 'It has been one of our bonuses since he became captain,' said Saville. This is not to say Gooch would wish to discard older players prematurely: he is a firm believer in rewarding individuals who have done well for the club. Essex have been able to afford to retain the likes of Keith Pont and David East until they have had Benefits. 'When Graham comes to have a Testimonial he will not push out a Beneficiary if their years coincide,' said Edwards.

Before taking the field, Gooch's team-talks with his Essex players would run along the lines of: 'This club's got a winning reputation. I don't want to see heads go down.' A few expletives are thrown in. His captaincy still tended to be inflexible: if Fletcher had a point to make (and Gooch would have liked him still to be on the field), then Gooch would change his mind. Otherwise it had to be someone whose opinions he rated highly. That person would have to know his subject. Derek Pringle, who had been appointed vice-captain, left Gooch alone unless he felt something was glaringly obvious; Neil Foster, on the other hand, had no shortage of opinions.

Gooch's resonant belief in physical fitness left no room for infidels. It was taken to extremes, especially pre-season. 'If anyone didn't agree with it, Graham would say: "Go and play somewhere else,"' said Pringle. Fletcher, although of the opinion that something other than merely a seven-mile run was required in training, was in support of this regimen; and even David Acfield, the club chairman designate, who would have hated such exertion, accepted that the game had changed. Gooch would insist on fielding practice every day – not that his views on this had altered over a decade: he had suggested to Mike Brearley in Australia that more slip-catching practice should be held before play began. Dedication and dedication to fitness had enhanced his own game, and his unwavering viewpoint was that it would assist everyone else.

Through arriving earlier at the ground and, indeed, practising earlier, Gooch was able to devote more time to the extraneous matters that burden a captain. He is not one to oversleep: rising between six and six-thirty each day gives him ample time to prepare himself. In his first spell as Essex captain the inference had been that captaincy had affected his batting, but he regarded the reverse as being the case. He found that by altering his routine he could cope with all the demands made of him. His batting for Essex bore this out, as it had done when he captained them when Fletcher stood down in 1988.

In his initial seven first-class matches in 1989, Gooch never made less than a half-century. In an important match against Middlesex at Chelmsford he scored the only half-century, making 65 out of a total of 149 on a pitch of low bounce. Essex won by nine wickets. He scored his first century of the season against Derbyshire, which led to another resounding victory. On a lively pitch at Bristol, he again made the sole half-century of their match against Gloucestershire, which resulted in a further victory. No one else scored more than 32. The contentious Reader ball with its high seam was proving lethal in the right hands.

Essex were at the top of the championship and faring well in the Sunday League and Benson & Hedges Cup by the time Gooch was chosen by England for their one-day matches against the touring Australians. He started propitiously, scoring 52 at Old Trafford, where he opened with Gower, 10 in a tied contest at Trent Bridge and his seventh international limited-overs century at – inevitably – Lord's. He struck eleven fours in making 136 off 162 balls in a high-scoring match which England lost. He was named England's Man of the Series. At this point there was no inkling of difficulties to come.

Unbeknown, though, to the Test and County Cricket Board and the International Cricket Council, as it was now styled, a tour to South Africa was in the offing. Already this was being furtively planned. It was inevitable, perhaps, after the cancellation of England's tour to India. That this had a bearing on the performances of those who also played for England during the summer was equally inevitable.

As one of England's leading cricketers and, of course, the captain of the 1982 tour to South Africa, Gooch's name was prominent among those whom the South African Cricket Union would have wished to attract. John Emburey, who remained his closest friend within cricket, was recruiting players and naturally would have wished to have Gooch with him. If the timing of the tour proved to be awry politically, so it was from the standpoint of the organisers. For Gooch was in the process of bringing a libel action against the *Daily Mirror*, who had published a story alleging that Gooch – and eight others – had already signed to play in South Africa. Gooch maintained he had not been approached and received support from Ali Bacher and Joe Pamensky. The matter was settled out of court, Gooch receiving £20,000 plus costs in damages. Would he have gone to the Republic otherwise? 'I would rather not say whether I would have gone had I been asked,' he said. 'I can't say how I would have reacted had I been offered £200,000.'

It transpired that the *Daily Mirror* had done Gooch – and English cricket – a good turn. Needless to say, Gooch has never had a notably friendly relationship with any journalist from either the *Daily Mirror* or the *Sun*, the other newspaper to have libelled him. 'The journalists who get further with me are the ones who build up a friendly relationship,' he said. He could have added that those who cross him are lucky if he speaks to them again.

Gooch would not have wanted to put himself and his family through the opprobrium that would undoubtedly have arisen again from another such tour. There were two other overriding reasons why he might well have turned down an approach. He was sufficiently well off and, whatever his reservations about touring, was well aware that his Test average was not what it should have been. He had, of course, missed a possible thirty-one Tests through his ban at a time when he was supposedly in his prime. Although he was thirty-six during the summer of 1989, he felt there were still a few years left in him at the highest level. 'I want to be proud of my performances when I retire, and an important part of that concerns an improvement in my Test record,' he said. 'I have thrown away a few centuries by getting out in the seventies and eighties and I would not want to go out of the game having scored less than double figures in hundreds. I would like to be averaging over forty in Tests – at the moment my Test record is no more than OK.'

As Fletcher pointed out, Gooch now realised he was potentially a great batsman.

David Norrie felt Gooch definitely did not want to go again. Insole said that Gooch 'hated the criticism which came from his family. He was more established and wanted to go on playing for England, but I don't think he saw then that he could become England captain again.' Lever thought differently: 'He obviously wanted the captaincy of England.' To Pringle, Gooch is 'quietly ambitious – but he would not admit it'. Such conflicting views from those outside his family who knew him best were summed up by Norrie: 'You think you know him – but even then you don't know him at all.'

Nevertheless, when the sixteen names of what became known as Mike Gatting's party were leaked to the press – on the day Australia regained the Ashes – there was widespread surprise that Gooch was not among them. For by then he had completely lost his form at Test level. He had also found the England side of that summer to be the most dispirited he had ever played in. 'Playing for Essex had left its mark on him because everyone was trying his hardest. The matches were small, humorous affairs which were very important to him. Perhaps he resented it when he did not find this at England level,' said Peter Roebuck. When his cricket with England was not going well, as it was not that summer, Gooch, it was felt, tended to hark back to his county. Some Essex players seemed to encourage this, possibly the upshot of Fletcher having been sacked by England.

Having won the toss in the first Test at Headingley and put Australia in, England lost by 210 runs. Gooch's contributions were 13, and 68 out of an ignominious second-innings total of 191: this was to be his highest score of the series. Both times he was out lbw, first to

Terry Alderman, who delivered the ball especially close to the stumps, and then to Merv Hughes. His difficulty was countering at Test level swing bowling that, especially in the case of Alderman, was high-class. His batting prior to that had been on ordinary county pitches against bowlers who did not attempt to swing the ball, but merely relied on utilising the high seam.

Gooch usually tended to play around his front pad when out of form, although that was not the case at this stage of the series. Insole, for one, reckoned this was a technical failing which came when he adopted his high stance. He was committing himself early to play off the front foot to counter seam bowling at county level, which did not help his game in Test cricket. His forward movement may, as Angus Fraser suggested, have been exacerbated by Alderman taking an unusually long run-up for a bowler of his pace. Batsmen were deceived into thinking he would be quicker than he was.

In the second Test at Lord's, again won by Australia, Gooch made 60 in the first innings, his nineteenth half-century in his last eighteen first-class matches. In the second innings he was out again to Alderman, lbw in the first over of the innings. This was Alderman's hundredth Test wicket, and Australia won comfortably. By now Gooch's form was affected at county level, a run of low scores being relieved by a solitary century against Leicestershire.

Australia again had the better of the third Test at Edgbaston, which was rain-affected. Once more Gooch was out lbw, this time to Geoff Lawson, for 8. That he was now having difficulty making any score of note had much to do with the field-placings Australia had adopted since the first of the limited-overs internationals. 'We noticed his tendency to play through mid-wicket and decided to put one or two fielders in attacking positions on the on side,' said Bobby Simpson, their manager. 'This made it difficult for Graham to score and harder also in that he would have to look for other areas to make his runs. We created doubt in his mind and over his peculiar front-foot movement with the result that his performances did not match his potential. There was not a lot of movement but always a chance of dismissing him by keeping the ball on his off stump. Most of the wickets Terry Alderman obtained were with the ball that nipped back.'

Even taking into account that the best batsmen are more likely to be lbw or caught in the slips than bowled when facing the new ball, there was no doubting that Gooch was out lbw an inordinate number of times. Throughout his career this has been a regular mode of dismissal. As well as playing round the front leg he did not move his left foot a long way down the pitch, preferring instead to shift his weight from one foot to the other. Thus some umpires were less inclined to give him the benefit of the doubt with lbw decisions. Certainly, there were occasions in 1989 when he looked to be unfortunate to be given out to the Australian medium-pacers – and, as he himself pointed out, plenty of other batsmen were dismissed by Alderman. In fact, of Alderman's forty-one wickets in the series, nineteen were through lbw decisions. Gooch had to counter a habit of committing himself on the front foot against swing bowling: he favoured the advice of Geoff Boycott and Alan Knott, who were assisting with the England coaching, rather than the opinions of the Essex staff. By the following summer, instead of going back and across his stumps, he would put the front edge of his back pad just outside leg stump to avoid playing across his front pad.

Gooch's sequence of low scores continued in the fourth

Test at Old Trafford, where Australia retained the Ashes. He was neither out lbw nor dismissed by Alderman but mustered only 11 and 13 and opted to be dropped for the fifth Test, which was to start only nine days later. No player contracted to tour South Africa was included, either; not that this made any difference. Australia still won, and by an innings and 180 runs. Gooch saw no point in his inclusion now that the destiny of the Ashes was settled and was peeved when the England committee brought back in his place Martyn Moxon, then twenty-nine and out of form, rather than a younger opening batsman. 'I said that with the Ashes lost there was now an opportunity to have a look at another opener, especially as I was not playing well,' he said. 'I was disappointed because I had hoped to get a couple of hundreds to take me up to ten in Tests. If the selectors had really forced the issue, then I would have played. But I just did not merit my place in the side. I cannot see how that should ever suggest I was being selective about when I should play.' It was characteristic that he should feel the need for more, not less cricket. The drawback, he felt, about playing Test cricket as a batsman was that he would not have enough innings during a season. 'After each five-day Test it seems you just have two one-day matches and, if you are lucky, one three-day match before you report back with England. If you have had a poor Test and your confidence is low, this is of little use in putting things right.'

Gooch was convinced that the county championship needed different scheduling. At the time he was fully in support of a championship of sixteen four-day matches, which his own county committee had always vehemently opposed. 'I have changed my view on this,' he admitted. 'I am no longer against four-day fixtures as games of cricket. I can only speak as a player but I have come round to the opinion that they are a truer test of a team and give batsmen the chance to build innings,' he said. 'If we are to go over completely to a four-day programme, it must be structured so that the Test players are available for the great majority of championship games.'

He found some form, not that in the various domestic competitions he had ever really been out of it. Since the first Test he had amassed 659 runs for Essex in all their cricket at an average of 65. Against Worcestershire in Colchester week at the start of August he made 51 out of 208 and then 17 in the second innings. In the second match he took 75 off Northamptonshire, reaching his half-century before his opening partner, John Stephenson, had achieved double figures. This was followed by 68 against Lancashire and a half-century against the Australians for Essex. Others might have stood down from such a match in his circumstances; not Gooch. He was unable to stave off a further victory by the Australians, making 21 in the second innings as Essex were dismissed for 205, yet he felt in sufficient touch not to object to his inclusion in the sixth and final Test at the Oval. He was deluded. Australia made another massive total (468), in reply to which England lost a wicket in their very first over: Gooch lbw bowled Alderman 0.

Alderman had had his successes bowling against Gooch in the 1981 Tests, and for Kent and Gloucestershire at county level, but before this series had not attempted to restrict his scoring through this positioning of a short mid-wicket as well as a fieldsman in a conventional mid-wicket position. 'In the one-day match at Old Trafford I saw Graham was hitting the ball in the air, and by putting the two men in close we made him think. It was his run-scoring area. All batsmen go through bad patches

– in the past when I've bowled at him and he has been on top he has whacked the ball to the boundary,' said Alderman. 'But he is a batsman who is not at home when he is not striking the ball and the scoreboard is not ticking over. That summer he was not playing as straight as he should have been and didn't know where his stumps and feet were, although he was starting to get it right by the end of the series. The doubt was put in his mind by mixing the ball that cut back with the away-swingers.'

In five Tests, Gooch compiled only 183 runs. There was inevitable criticism of his high backlift, the insinuation being that his bat was not coming down straight. Knott thought its value to him was not so much in the pick-up, but as a means of geeing himself up as the bowler ran in. But it was blindingly clear how much he preferred the ball to come on to the bat, as when he played the West Indies. He still felt his timing to be out of sorts come the autumn, when he took part in the Nehru Cup in India. And yet his batting in the championship did not falter at the end of the season. In his final innings he made 158 against Leicestershire, his highest score of a tantalisingly mixed year. He finished with an average of 52 in the championship, which Essex really should have won.

In July they were leading the championship table as well as the Sunday League. They had also reached the final of the Benson & Hedges Cup, which they lost to Nottinghamshire off the very last ball. Gooch contributed 48 off sixty-three balls to an Essex total of 243 for 7. He then conceded 57 runs off his allotted eleven overs. Entrusting the last over of the match to Lever, Nottinghamshire needing 9 to win, he took a calculated risk, placing all but one fielder on the leg side. Yet, against the odds, Eddie Hemmings made sufficient room to squeeze the ball to the backward-point boundary. There was further disappointment in the Sunday League owing to Essex having their penultimate match of the season abandoned. Victory over Lancashire, the eventual winners, would have taken them back to the top of the table. A further 83 runs were needed from 17.2 overs before rain stopped play. When it ceased and the covers had been removed without undue hurry, the umpires decreed that there was insufficient time for the match to be completed. In the NatWest Trophy, Essex faltered in the first round, in spite of Gooch making 94 in their tie against Somerset. No other Essex player made more than 24. Most frustrating of all, though, was the docking of 25 points by the Test and County Cricket Board for a substandard pitch at Southend which had been prepared not by the Essex groundsman but by the local council. Both matches in Southend week were won by Essex, but the penalty left them with −3 points from their victory over Yorkshire; as a result Worcestershire regained the championship by six points.

Gooch's strange season was not finished yet. It was inevitable that Gower would not be retained to captain England in the West Indies that winter. Australia had heaped humiliation upon his sides to the extent that the players had become utterly dispirited. Changes had to be made. But, with Gatting having opted to lead the tour to South Africa, there was a shortage of likely captains. Some favoured a captain who had not been implicated in the summer débâcle. In a lunchtime radio discussion during the NatWest final, three national newspaper journalists each plumped for an outsider: Ian Greig, Phil Neale and Peter Roebuck were the three names put forward. Yet once the England committee decided that the Caribbean was not the place to blood a captain whose place in the team was unproven, a swift process of elimination narrowed the choice to one man.

Gooch did not demur when offered the captaincy. He had never wanted to lose it and yet he did not seek it, either. He told Norrie that he would not be able to resume it if he was worried about losing it. Of greater concern was his Test record. If he was to improve on it, he could not afford to miss another tour, even one to the West Indies. Bob Willis, assistant manager on the 1986 tour, felt Gooch showed 'a lot of fortitude' in returning.

Gooch determined to improve England's cricket in at least one respect: their pride. He was well aware he was the third–choice captain but, since he was no prima donna, did not let that concern him. He did not want anyone under his leadership treating playing for his country as just another day at the office. He bore no grudges against Ted Dexter for his personal criticism, even though he would not have tolerated it from an ordinary journalist. Their relationship was accommodating, if distant. They were two shy men. 'There was no lingering nastiness, but it was quite something for Graham to overcome being compared to a wet fish,' said Insole. Dexter felt that his article did not make their relationship a difficult one – 'or it did not appear to do so'. The chairman also stood by his original appointment of Gower as captain instead of Gooch. 'It was not a mistake. The point was that Graham was an inexperienced captain and David had won a home series against Australia in the past.'

The touring party included one surprise and one shock: no Gower and no Botham. Gooch did not have much say in this, partly no doubt because he was not entrenched as captain. Poignantly, he was in a position to inform Gower in person. The occasion was the first day of the end–of–season match between Essex and Leicestershire.

Gooch scored a century; Gower was out for a duck, although he did manage a compensating century in Leicestershire's second innings. 'I appreciated Graham's honesty on what must have been an embarrassing matter,' said Gower. 'A week earlier I had been his England captain. Now, here he was telling me I was no longer wanted in his England team.'

Had Gooch decided to retire from Test cricket when he requested to be omitted from the fifth Test – as well he might have done – how would his career epitaph have read? Writing in *The Times*, Alan Lee reckoned that under-achievement would have been its theme 'along with muted words about leadership limitations and an introverted personality whose barriers could tend towards paranoia'.

Mickey Stewart, however, would not have agreed with Lee's assessment. He was one of the few people who felt Gooch had more to offer than his seemingly humdrum persona suggested, feeling that his public image was far from the whole truth.

In October their joint emphasis on the work ethic was apparent when England took part in the Nehru Cup, a one-day tournament staged to celebrate the birth of India's first prime minister after independence. Captain and manager, dubbed 'the cockney Mafia', were in accord as to their task and the remedy for defeat: work, work and still more work. The party which was destined for the West Indies went to India for three weeks. Gower and Botham having been left behind, too closely linked with a defeatist era, there was the chance for the management to impart its own ethos. Gooch and Stewart saw eye to eye to the extent that in England they would meet socially with their wives (something that Gooch has never done with Dexter); but Stewart bridles at the suggestion that he hits it off better with Gooch than Gower because of greater similarity in their backgrounds. 'Surely, I'm closer in background to David than to Graham,' he protested.

What Stewart particularly appreciated about Gooch was his strength of character – 'those consecutive noughts in 1987 were character-building' – and his 'leadership from the front', a cliché perhaps, but apposite. For England, the Nehru Cup, although yet another one-day exercise, was important to their long-term plans in that it was something more than a get-together at Lilleshall. They did sufficiently well in the six-nation competition to reach the semi-finals, in which they lost to Pakistan. Gooch himself made 5 against Sri Lanka and then 56 in a seven-wicket victory over Australia, playing Alderman, his demon of the summer, with something approaching confidence. He had not 'complicated things' by studying videos of himself batting against Alderman. 'I don't feel in as good nick as I would like but you get confidence in the middle and until you have had a long knock you are never 100 per cent happy.' The notion of Gooch being 100 per cent happy was a novel one to Simon Barnes, reporting for *The Times*.

He followed this by making 7 and, more important, returning his best one-day international figures of 10–4–19–3 in a four-wicket win over Pakistan (he raised his arms aloft at the pleasure of bowling Javed Miandad); then 21 in a defeat by India and 59 against the West Indies in a match England also lost. They chose to spend their day off flying to Nagpur for the semi-final against Pakistan, arriving too late for a session in the Nagpur Stadium and hence frustrating dedicated workers and pleasure-seekers alike. Gooch made 35 but did not bowl in a rain-affected match which Pakistan won comfortably.

During the Nehru Cup, graffiti was spotted which read 'Thatcher out' and, scrawled underneath, 'lbw b Alderman'. That was the extent of the humiliation wreaked upon England and Gooch during the summer. Now they had made a start, if only a start, on regaining some esteem. No one took his cricket more seriously in these three weeks than Gooch, and yet his early years with Essex had not been forgotten. He remained emphatic that it was still possible to crack a joke in the middle. Allan Border, in the midst of making a violent unbeaten 84 off just forty-four balls in England's match against Australia, smote Angus Fraser for a couple of sixes. Fraser suggested to Gooch that he try a slower ball, which prompted a laugh. Neither did Gooch lead a totally bland life off the field. He had been to India before and enjoyed what he saw of the country and its culture. 'He is not a guy who will shy away from different experiences if they are offered to him,' said Derek Pringle. Yet he went prepared. In addition to his surplus batteries for his cassette recorder (he always has a surplus), half a dozen bottles of red wine survived the X-ray scanner on the way out. Allan Lamb had come similarly equipped.

As for politics, there was no objection to his presence. He had, after all, decided not to return to South Africa and made the right noises about enjoying his cricket in India. During the tournament his name was taken off the United Nations blacklist, along with more than 300 other sportsmen who had South African connections of one sort or another. These included Lamb. The deletions, the largest ever to have been made, followed pledges by the International Cricket Council and the International Motorcycling Federation to take action against athletes who continued to take part in events in the Republic.

The ICC would introduce bans from Test cricket even on those planning to coach there.

Asked shortly afterwards whether he was still keeping his options open over playing in South Africa again, Gooch parried the question. 'I know that, if I want to play there, that would be the end of my Test career – and at the moment I would like it to continue,' he said. 'I am disappointed at the restrictions to discourage English cricketers from going there. The younger players will miss valuable coaching and playing opportunities and the chance to help Black and Coloured cricketers. I feel that a citizen of the UK should be allowed to go there without being punished. Sport is such an easy touch for the politicians. I do not agree with apartheid. It is a terrible system but the cricketers out there are doing their best to put things right. I have never had one cross word with any Coloured cricketer and their governments are perfectly entitled to take whatever stand they wish. But our cricketers are being victimised.'

There was further preparation for the West Indies in the form of more indoor practice and specialist coaching at Lilleshall. Players were told to prepare as never before. They were given new standards of fitness to achieve, as if they were seeking not bodily strength but moral vindication. Not for nothing did Fletcher, who had joined the ranks of England coaches, describe Gooch as the hardest-working cricketer he had seen – some praise considering he was a contemporary of Geoff Boycott.

8

The Ecstasy and the Agony

On account of his grim words on the air or in the press, his reserved demeanour and apparent lack of charisma, Gooch was underestimated. Those who know him within the game emphasise the correlation between his success as captain and as batsman, with a consequent developing of maturity and self-confidence. This was not readily apparent before the West Indies tour. 'The fact that he works hard and performs in the middle is important to the players under him – and is a factor of captaincy which is often forgotten,' said Bob Willis. 'Graham always leads by example and takes a level phlegmatic view. He never takes the game for granted, realising it usually has the last word.' He gained respect through never asking any player to do anything he would not do himself, and within the freemasonry of professional cricketers that was valued as highly as was tactical expertise. He would not criticise a player for not wearing a jacket and tie to a function and then fail to do so himself the following week. 'With Gatt you can say something to him if he tells you you're scruffy. You can have a go back. With Graham you can't as he's so well turned out,' said Angus Fraser.

Like every other captain Gooch had a clear picture of certain players he would like to have in his sides. That there was room for the gifted but unpredictable cricketer as well as the work-horse was evidenced in the selection of the touring party for the Nehru Cup and the West Indies. Wayne Larkins, an opener whose power and belligerence Gooch had long admired, was given a further chance to show that he could make something of his unquestioned ability. Gooch had seen enough, too, of Nasser Hussain to know that he likewise had a rare talent. The remainder of the party might have selected themselves had there not been an alternative tour. Doubtless Gooch would have liked to have John Emburey as his vice-captain – as would have been the case had the 1988 tour to India gone ahead – only he was contracted to play in South Africa. Allan Lamb, whose character Gooch spent a good deal of time working out, was to be vice-captain instead. A chance was taken with the pace bowlers, four of whom were West Indian born. When Dexter explained the policy as 'fighting fire with fire', there was little reaction other than guffaws. The Test figures of Devon Malcolm (or Malcolm Devon as the chairman once memorably called him) were 1 for 161. The Gooch–Stewart selection policy came to be based on consistency of performance: here Malcolm and Ricardo Ellcock were the exceptions. 'Otherwise', said the team manager, 'you don't know what you're getting.' The eleven best players, he felt, did not necessarily comprise the best side to put on the field.

From the outset Gooch spent much of his time with Stewart. He would, though, keep himself to himself in that the players found him still to be shy. He would not make a remark for its own sake. He would make an effort to go out with all the players in groups in the evening, and listen to what they had to say, not taking the high-handed attitude of the old pro. In the absence of Emburey he found a soulmate in David Norrie, who in spite of writing for the *News of the World*, hardly a favourite newspaper of cricketers, had become a friend of Emburey's and hence came to know Gooch. They would dine twice a week in the Caribbean, their relationship developing to the extent that Peter Roebuck reckoned the key to understanding Gooch was to understand Norrie, an extroverted Scot of similar age. The basis of their friendship was loyalty, the clear understanding being that any journalistic breach would put an end to it. 'To come into his company was a gradual process. He is a careful judge of character and, if anything, too loyal. We don't see eye to eye over a lot of people. But it is not as if he tells me a lot of confidences – it is not that kind of friendship,' said Norrie.

Gooch has need of a constant companion. Brenda came out to the Caribbean, but not until the party had reached Antigua. In some respects he might have been helped by having an outsider, rather than Emburey, as a friend on tour. Captaincy has always been a lonely task, and Gooch was now considerably older than the majority of the team. The captain's allegiance to Emburey, a player of similar age, might have been seen as an older-generation clique.

Once the tour was under way, Gooch did not appear to be homesick. There was hardly time to be. Every waking hour was filled. Owing to his early starts and, perhaps, to encroaching middle age, he would be falling asleep by 8.30 after a day in the field. He would order room service, watch a video and go to bed. Reading-matter would not be cerebral: most of his paperbacks would be thrillers. He insisted no one tell him the ending of the book *Red October*. His tastes in popular music, like those in wine and beer, had been influenced by Derek

Pringle, although he eschewed some of Pringle's more esoteric choices alongside Brenda's favourite Cliff Richard.

Gooch's attitude to the media was not as astringent as before: here Norrie had had a part to play. Whether camped by the hotel pool or the bar, England players of the 1980s mixed less with the press and broadcasters than they had in the past. Influenced by Norrie, Gooch did make the effort – 'and it was an effort,' said Norrie – to go into the press-box at St Kitts soon after the start of the tour. The journalists knew where they stood and, as Hussain discovered when he disputed a decision during the same match against the Leeward Islands, so did the players. He was officially reprimanded by captain and management. Gooch's tolerance does not extend to those under him not abiding by the umpire's ruling. This was the first incident of any sort on the tour, which had otherwise begun well. Gooch had made 46 and 50, and England batted consistently overall, Larkins and Stewart both making centuries. The second match against Windward Islands was lost, but only just, and that more through a lack of match practice than ineffectual cricket.

There were to be two one-day internationals in Trinidad prior to the first Test. Only four years had passed since Gooch had been greeted there with a burning effigy and placards portraying him as a cricketer who upheld apartheid. Now, just as in India, there was no opposition to his presence. England, it was true, were warned not to stray from their hotel or the ground at Port of Spain; but this was to avoid muggings rather than demonstrators. Both matches were severely restricted by rain, which gave them just one further three-day contest in which to prepare for the first Test. That was if batting against Jamaica's spinners could be considered the best way to prepare for the West Indies attack on one of the fastest pitches in the world. Jamaica withdrew all three of their Test players, two of them fast bowlers. At any rate, Gooch made the most of winning the toss and of the circumstances. He batted for 286 minutes in making 239, his highest score on an England tour. There were five sixes and thirty-one fours, mostly taken off the spinners. He retired hurt on 222, authentically so since he was suffering from cramp, but was soon able to resume. Those who saw the innings regarded it as one of the more violent he had played in recent years, as a throwback to the time when he pulverised attacks. Playing the percentages, as cricketers were wont to say, could disguise mediocrity or, in Gooch's case, the slowing-down of the body; but it made for a duller game.

In one further respect, Gooch prepared thoroughly for the series. Always meticulous over his equipment, he was the first batsman to have a Velcro strip fitted to the inside of his thigh pad so that he could fix an attachable piece of towelling to soak up sweat. Then he could pull it off and wash it. The majority of county cricketers would merely leave their sweat-soaked thigh pads to dry in the sun during intervals, which meant they were in an unhygienic state come the end of the season. Gooch could not accept this, and neither could Allan Border, who soon copied his friend's idea.

Even the West Indies, the most successful and complete cricket side in the world, could not match Gooch's attention to detail, practice and fitness, which now was to pay in the most handsome way. They crucially underestimated England, not least because they had not lost a Test to them since 1974. On the last occasion the two sides played at Sabina Park, in 1986, the pitch was so spiteful that Gooch had feared for his safety for the only time in his career. This pitch proved to be sporting, only in a different sense. The most surprising aspect was that it helped the medium-pacers, of whom England had three, as well as the genuine fast bowlers, of whom the West Indies had plenty. Never can a side have been so strongly backed to win a Test match as the West Indies were now; and yet they failed lamentably.

If their attitude was complacent, so, too, were most aspects of their game. They mustered 164 in their first innings, their lowest total against England for twenty-one years, having been 62 without loss. In effect Gooch was required to rotate his four bowlers, of whom only Malcolm was genuinely fast – and surprisingly accurate – but his tactics were deemed positive as well as considerate. He did like to have his own way with field placings. Fraser, who bowled with commendable control and success, taking 5 for 28, would rather bowl to a relatively defensive field on flat pitches – 'I perform better if I can clamp the batsman down' – but found Gooch to have decided views of his own. On this occasion, at least, attacking the batsman succeeded. What was more, England, having lost Gooch to Patrick Patterson for 18, managed to gain a first-innings lead of exactly 200 through a century by Lamb and 57 from Robin Smith. Gooch had been caught at the wicket off an authentic leg glance, a mode of dismissal that has afflicted him more in county cricket than in Test matches.

The West Indies batted better in their second innings but not a great deal better; Malcolm, bowling with unsuspected hostility, and Gladstone Small, concentrating on a steady line, took four wickets apiece. England were left with just 41 to win, and not even the loss of the fourth day's play to rain and the dismissal of Gooch for 8, this time to Ian Bishop, could prevent them from winning by nine wickets. It was one of the most memorable victories in the history of Test cricket and celebrated as vividly as any. No one was more drunk that night than Gooch in the Pegasus Hotel. Photographs of him smiling are few and far between, and the one in colour that graced the cover of the *Cricketer* the following month captured him in as radiant a mood as the public has ever seen him.

If any one day can be said to have radically altered the public's perception of Gooch, it was that final day at Sabina Park. There were impressive personal feats to come, but this was acclaimed rapturously from the Prime Minister to Mike Denness, captain when England last beat the West Indies all those years ago, and the man who at one time would have reacted with disbelief to the prospect of Gooch becoming England captain. Now the momentum had to be maintained. There was another of the endless round of one-day internationals to be played two days later on the same ground. It could so easily have been anticlimactic. In fact it reached a thrilling conclusion, the West Indies winning off the very last ball. Gooch made 2, which he followed with 33 in the fourth match of the one-day series, played in Guyana. This, too, was won by the West Indies, which meant they had an unassailable two–nil lead.

For the next week, England were marooned. The ground at Georgetown was waterlogged. For the third time on an England tour, there would not be a ball bowled in the Guyana Test. Far from feeling gratitude that England's lead was protected, as was suggested in some quarters, Gooch was concerned lest his players lose the impetus that their victory in Kingston had given them. An extra one-day international was arranged for what would have been the final day of the Test and this, too, was won by the West Indies. Gooch contributed 42 to a lacklustre performance. When England finally escaped Guyana, they found that their enforced rest had indeed done their game no good at all; yet still they managed to beat a President's Eleven by 113 runs in southern Trinidad. Gooch's own form was commanding. He made 66 and 61, dismissed in each innings by a leg-spinner, Robert Haynes. England won the match through more venomous pace bowling from Malcolm.

Such a result enabled England to approach the third Test, at Port of Spain, with increased confidence. They had to demonstrate that their victory at Kingston had not been illusory and, helped by winning the toss, they were soon doing just that. Gooch opted to bowl first as a positive rather than a defensive measure on a pitch which was well grassed and proved to be uneven in bounce. Again, England's seamers were mightily impressive. The West Indies collapsed to 29 for 5 before Gus Logie, returning from injury, effected a recovery with Carl Hooper. This was all the more vital since Richards had dropped out of their side owing to a recurrence of his haemorrhoid trouble. They finished with a total of 199. Gooch in reply was in his most circumspect mood, putting on 112 with Larkins in fifty-three overs – and those bowled at a funereal eleven an hour. Such self-denial, considering that both batsmen essentially liked to attack, must have been almost purgatory. At the end of the second day Gooch remained unbeaten on 83. The next morning, though, he added only a single before he was taken at the wicket off a lifting ball from Bishop. He had batted for 6½ hours and given England the vital start. The West Indies, however, were swiftly back in the match, dismissing England for 288 before Malcolm showed again that his selection had been inspired. He took six of the West Indians' second-innings wickets for 77, including three in four balls. England were left needing 151 to win and most of an – apparently – cloudless final day in which to make them.

The pitch was starting to deteriorate. In a sense, so, too, did the West Indian bowling, for it was short and wayward. Larkins soon went, caught at the wicket off Ezra Moseley, who then unwittingly changed the face of the series. Twice he struck Gooch on the left hand, causing him to retire after much prodding by Laurie Brown, England's physio, that made for another famous, vivid photograph: the captain was in agony. Taken to hospital, he was diagnosed as having broken a bone, although this was not revealed for fear of giving West Indies morale a boost. Upon returning to the ground, Gooch became more concerned with the unrelenting rain, which had been beating down since lunch. There was no respite until the match was all but over. When play eventually did restart, thirty overs remained for England to make 78 – on the face of it a straightforward task. This, though, was the Caribbean, where the light fades fast and where over rates do not accord with International Cricket Council stipulations. In nearly two hours the West Indies cynically bowled only sixteen overs in conditions barely fit for play. With five wickets remaining, thirty runs still required and darkness descending, England abandoned the chase. They did so amid confusion, for the signals from the dressing-room seemed to be unclear. Gooch's injury had left England bewildered, rudderless even. They were deflated. The high point of the tour had been passed.

Gooch had never broken a finger before. Remarkably, he had never missed a match for Essex or England through injury. Now he knew he would not take any further part in the tour. That evening he had dinner with

Norrie, who was astonished at his buoyancy. 'You would never have seen the West Indies again had they lost,' said Norrie. 'And yet in spite of it all Graham was so positive.' Gooch could not cope, though, when two tourists came across to their table to ask him whom he was dining with. He looked blank.

Such was the interest in England's remarkable perform-ances and in Gooch himself that he was starting to assume an almost mystical quality, as had Mike Brearley almost a decade before. The inner self was the subject of conjec-ture. Gooch was said to work out people's characters in the seclusion of his hotel room. His natural reserve enhanced his mystique, which even close friends such as Alan Lilley could not penetrate. He had reached maturity and near-greatness as a cricketer, but had not necessarily done so as an individual. Tabloid newspapers are apt to label a great cricketer as 'the great man' when in actuality he is nothing of the kind.

To the public, most of the press and even some of his colleagues, Gooch remained the riddle wrapped in the mystery inside the enigma. He knew about his image, did not necessarily like it but shrugged it off. 'I'm too old to change,' he said. It was as if he was not yet accepted, even though seven years had elapsed since his South African venture. 'He was the arch-rebel who had still to become Goody Two-Shoes,' was how Phil Edmonds described him. Peter Roebuck saw in him a curious mix of 'outlaw and patriot'. To cricket followers he was dogged, imperturbable, inexpressive. Even Gooch himself realised that nobody could possibly imagine he enjoyed playing. 'I know I look a totally mis-erable sod out there. I wish I didn't. But there you are. If only they knew, for I enjoy it all right. I truly love the game. I suppose I must appear a bit staid, a bit dour, keeping my emotions in check. Certainly in these image-conscious days it pays to blow your own trumpet a little rather than sit back and let things come your way, like I do. Perhaps my posture has something to do with it. I have inherited my dad's rounded shoulders. My sense of humour is not the back-slapping, bellow-laughter style; I prefer a quiet dig without being effervescent. I just haven't got a very out-going public image, but ask any-one in the dressing-room and I reckon they'd say I laugh and joke and am just as comradely a team man as anyone else.'

Gooch admitted he still felt shy and inhibited when he was recognised wherever he went. Dexter was not exclusive in his opinion that Gooch did not have a great deal of charisma, and yet his captain made no attempt to cultivate it through adopting a full-time agent or a part-time image. Not for him pantomime roles that Ian Botham took on or nightclub appearances that were the prerogative of the successful sportsman; it was not his style. He paid attention to how he dressed without fol-lowing any particular fashion. His only conscious affecta-tion was his long-standing fickle affair with his razor, rotating through beard, designer stubble and a clean-shaven look. 'There were times in his bleaker phases when it seemed a ruse to avoid recognition,' said Alan Lee. One bold attempt by another journalist to discover whether his non-shaving days were due to superstition or a sensitive skin was met with a curt 'Mind your own business'. In fact he is superstitious, as is his mother and his mother's sister. He believes in touching wood, and in the middle will not change his equipment, even if that needs doing, until he has scored at least twenty runs. The stubble? He regards it as a beard, and compares preference for a close shave with choosing lager ahead of beer.

His captaincy of England paid little homage to image. It was essentially no different from his leadership of Essex, except in one respect. Those who did not know him might have construed 'the huddle', as his team-talks on the field became known, as designed to impress anyone beyond the boundary. The England players would congregate in a tight ring after taking the field until, John Woodcock remarked sarcastically in *The Times*, 'one expected to see a pair of rugger shorts tossed out from among them'. Gone was the white waterfall as players cascaded down the pavilion steps and spread out to their places in the field. This public briefing had its origins on the 1990 tour of the West Indies, where the close proximity of the dressing-rooms meant that Gooch's pep-talks could sometimes be overheard. It was to become a regular feature of the Gooch–Stewart regime, even when England were playing at Lord's where a vast expanse of corridor separates the dressing-rooms.

There was little Churchillian rhetoric in these team-talks. 'I like people to enjoy their cricket and within that enjoyment I like them to give a hundred per cent,' said Gooch. 'I want them to know in their own minds where they are going. I want them to know what their job is and to prepare themselves for it properly. Cricket is a job of work and it's a game; the balance between those two things is important. You have to realise what you can do and what you can't do and, from there, how to organise your game. All these things are important and the people who work that out – in any walk of life – are usually successful. I want people who want to do well and try to be competitive. It's important to get the right kind of player. You've got to want it badly.'

For Gooch, the right kind of player did not include the

gifted dilettante. He was always going to have difficulty in incorporating in his sides David Gower, whom other colleagues felt he did not understand. There are few grey areas with Gooch. Talking about 'giving a hundred per cent' was football jargon to Gower; to Gooch the words carried an important meaning. They were charismatic words in team-talks and demanded respect. The respect of outsiders was of less importance. 'I'm not in the job for the kudos of being England captain,' he said. 'I want to do well for England. I want to win Test matches and perform well and compete. It we don't perform well, I don't like it. Defeat is part of your life as a sportsman. I like to win a lot but, more important to me, I like competing.'

Gooch was especially aware that, with the exception of Mike Brearley, the tenures of all the England captains of his time had reached sticky conclusions. This hardly made the England captaincy an attractive proposition. On the other hand, he could do no worse than his immediate predecessors who had taken sides to the Caribbean. No one seemed to think he was the right captain; and certainly no one expected him to do well. The belief was that his public utterances were too bland, too trite. The words were the comfortable clichés of sporting life. But there was nothing wrong with his philosophy: 'Captaincy is gelling the lads into a happy unit that performs; getting the best out of everyone by exhortation or example or both. Tactically, it's to do with experience, how wickets might play, how to prey on opposition weaknesses. The basics of setting fields are pretty standard really. Dynamic bowling changes are more to do with luck nine times out of ten.' When his old adversary, the *Sun*, stated after his first Test as captain that his leadership was 'safe and conservative', Gooch was amused that they claimed to know something about leadership. But he did not object.

Although Gooch was nearer middle age than youth, some felt it was conceivable he still had to realise his full potential away from the cricket field. 'Like a lot of cricketers Graham is not academic but is intelligent,' said Derek Pringle. 'He has an inquisitive mind and the capacity to be interested in many things.' Becoming captain of England had certainly heightened his awareness of the needs of others, even if he still looked upon captaincy through a batsman's eyes, and a preoccupied batsman at that. One England player felt that 'he cannot quite see round corners'. His qualities of leadership were not so well defined as his powers of motivation that stemmed from his own example, although Stewart was of the opinion that his tactical know-how was improving match by match. Even after two unhappy tours of the West Indies, on one of which England were well beaten and on the other annihilated, he had still convinced himself England could win; and he had transmitted this to his players. Once again he had shown impressive conviction in sticking to his beliefs. And he wished to be judged solely by results.

Although Lamb had now assumed the leadership, Gooch decided to stay on in the Caribbean and help where best he could. It was still his team. From Trinidad his entourage left for Barbados, where a makeshift England team that included Gower, temporarily forsaking his journalistic duties, drew with the island. In spite of being incapacitated, Gooch was still in demand from the press – who had found him to be helpful throughout the tour – and, now, a biographer. Mark Peel was in the Caribbean to research a study of Ken Barrington. Attempting to make polite small-talk to Gooch upon introducing himself, he said that England's one–nil lead in the series was 'a turn-up for the book' and was promptly denounced. Peel reminded him that before England left there had been suggestions that the tour be cancelled and that a certain Ian Botham had stated publicly England would lose five–nil. 'Well he was wrong, wasn't he?' said Gooch tersely. After that, they kept to the subject of Barrington.

Gooch's difficulty was in remaining as captain while Lamb gave the team-talks and made the relevant decisions. Gooch did not want to interfere; equally he wished to retain some influence. Lamb was still an inexperienced tactician, having succeeded Geoff Cook as Northamptonshire's captain only the previous season; and the Barbados Test was his first as England captain. His problems were compounded by injuries to his side, which would be taking on opponents bolstered by the return of Richards and by their narrow escape in Trinidad.

The loss of England's captain and leading batsman, followed by an injury in Barbados to Fraser, their most reliable bowler, proved decisive. They put the West Indies in and were thoroughly outclassed by a side that for once played to its full potential. The absence of Gooch also appeared to affect England's self-belief, even though Lamb could only be admired for his gutsy approach, epitomised in his second century of the series. Despite obdurate second-innings resistance from Russell and Smith West Indies won by 164 runs amid media allegations of gamesmanship by Richards which Lamb, Gooch and England's management wisely refrained from inflaming. The scheduling of the tour, devised with an eye to tourism, was such that the fifth and final Test in Antigua began just two days later, giving England scant opportunity to lick their wounds, literally as well as metaphorically. For Gooch, the end of a three-month tour was improved by the arrival of Brenda and their three children, complete with nanny in Karen Kaye, girlfriend and subsequently wife of Alan Lilley. Her decision to look after the children – while Lilley ran around Chelmsford in pre-season training – had been made after a trial weekend coping with them in Center Parcs at Thetford (and after a couple of bottles of wine). The idea was that they would all take a holiday following the Test. Florida was initially the favoured destination, but they settled on staying on in Antigua.

The tour was quickly extinguished. 'A series which had been richly competitive ended with a match which was so one-sided as to be anticlimactic,' wrote *Wisden*. On the quickest pitch of the series, which Andy Roberts, former West Indies fast bowler, had helped prepare, England were dismissed for 260 and 154, while West Indies dominated through an opening partnership of 298 between Gordon Greenidge, who made a century in his hundredth Test, and Desmond Haynes. England's bowlers lacked not only Gooch's firm leadership but also the discipline engendered from the start of the tour. The match was over in four days.

Gooch did not waste his time pondering on what might have been. He was pleased that England had shown they could compete with the best, even though their players were not as gifted. To him, this was not a surprise, even if it was to virtually everyone else. He knew more than most of the downs as well as the ups in a cricketer's career, not least as a result of England's two fruitless tours of the West Indies in the 1980s. Nothing could take away the fact that he had presided over the regaining of English cricket's self-respect. Gooch had rid England of the Botham-dominated team-within-a-team of the 1980s, with its boisterous off-field antics and snarling hostility towards the press. He had imbued a belief in practice that, to put it mildly, had not been a part of the 1986 tour. He believed passionately that the difference between ordinariness and excellence, the difference between England and the West Indies, could be made up by hard work. Even though the Wisden Trophy had not been regained, it was hard to find fault with his theory. He had reconstructed the England side and, in part, himself.

'We were not aware of how lucky we were going to be with Graham,' admitted Dexter, who had flown out to the Caribbean. 'He cared passionately about England. The impression I gained was that he had cricket on the mind all the time – work and family, and cricket is work. He said he could not handle players who were not making efforts to turn things round. I liked it when he said, "Only if you've done your level best to prepare yourself do you feel successful when you have achieved".'

9

Greatness Attained

The England captaincy was the making of Gooch. He was reappointed for the 1990 series against New Zealand just a week after returning home, though the position would have been his for both series that summer had he not requested to be made captain only for the first of them. He did not look upon the job as a sinecure and, although he had no intention of making a hash of it, would not have especially minded losing it. The limelight held no attraction for him. It was April, and the English season was under way; he had managed only a few days' holiday. How many venerable cricketers in his circumstances would have volunteered to play in a Sunday League match the day after arriving home, especially if they had still been nursing sore hands? His devotion to Essex was such that his vice-captain, Derek Pringle, reckoned he would play for them without being paid, so well did he feel they had treated him down the years. Essex pay all their players the same, which doubtless has had something to do with their team spirit and success; equally there was no doubting that several counties would be quite willing to pay Gooch considerably more. Conversely, he did not see anything unusual in his devout dedication to his county. 'Some players think they can save their best performances for Tests – I see it the other way round,' he said. 'And that way you get chosen for England.'

His injured hand still strapped up, he opened the batting in that first Refuge Assurance match, against Kent at Chelmsford. There was no respite from West Indian fast bowlers, Tony Merrick dismissing him for 3. Gooch also gave himself a bowl, five overs in a match Essex lost. Soon he was fully recovered and batting with remarkable consistency. There was no sense of anticlimax after the tour of the West Indies, no sense of having had a surfeit of cricket. A survey of cricket in the 1980s published that spring revealed Gooch to have scored more runs in first-class cricket (21,174) during the decade than any other batsman in the world. In 269 matches he had 465 innings and averaged 49.01. His 59 centuries were exceeded only by Viv Richards, who made 62 and had a slightly better average. The two had not stood comparison, even though they were of a similar age and had both been batsmen of unfettered power. Now, as Richards's interest and consequently his achievements were seemingly waning, Gooch was becoming increasingly prolific. He had more to prove.

Of other heavy run-scorers over the previous decade, Mike Gatting had a record which was almost on a par with Gooch's. He could well have been in Gooch's position of pre-eminence at the start of the 1990s had their careers not diverged, Gatting having gone to South Africa in a huff over his treatment by the Test and County Cricket Board and press alike. In their captaincy and approach to the game they have more in common than did either with David Gower. Gooch, taking nothing for granted, simplifies the game in his impassioned, if brief, team-talks. He is not one to overdo advice and yet he has conjured more out of his players than either of the other two. Gatting, more vociferous, likes to exude confidence and bravado. If the opposition does well, Gatting might say they were lucky and that his side had some bad decisions; in short, he is inclined to come up with excuses. Gooch is more of a realist, although less so than Gower, who presumes, like Mike Brearley, that if a player is good enough to play for England he knows what to do. Gooch, driven by insecurity, presumes nothing. He is, though, more inclined than Gatting to stand back and observe the spectacle unfolding in front of him. He now watches the ball all the way round the field, even when it is not coming near him – not something he would have contemplated in earlier years.

There is a fine line between Gooch's steadfastness and his stubbornness. Is it a seamer's day or a spinner's day? In a way he functions as a pack leader. He keeps bowlers on for long spells, a habit he picked up under Keith Fletcher. These tend to be his seamers. Naturally he wants to have his best bowlers on for most of the time, which means Neil Foster was given much to do. Gatting, who has voiced criticism of Gooch's handling of Angus Fraser, felt that Foster would bowl an over or two too many in a spell.

Gatting thinks Gooch's analysis in order to obtain the right balance of players is similar to that of Gower. They evaluate strengths and weaknesses. Gooch, Gatting feels, can impart to players exactly what he means. 'He might have learned that from Mike Brearley. He believes in what he says and gets across that he believes.' Gower feels that Gooch had become more professional and taken more pride in his performances. 'And Graham became more demonstrative in his expectations of others.' Because of his status and willingness to lead by example, fewer players have questioned his leadership. His Essex and England teams have grown devoted to him to the extent that they do not answer back. The Essex side of the 1990s is not so jolly as their counterparts a decade before; but every player adheres to their rigorous training schedules. There are no dissenting voices.

If Gooch feels a player is fully committed to Essex or England, he will stand up for him. He believes his success has sprung from hard work and has an inflexible attitude towards those not self-motivated. 'He can't suffer people who don't give everything like him,' said Graham Saville. He can be ruthless even towards those who do. It was not because Rob Bailey had let him down that he did not feature in his post-West Indies plans. Far from it. Gooch was simply not convinced he was good enough. Bailey would have to score a stack of runs in county cricket before being given another chance. As for Gower, he would dearly like to have him in his side for his rare talent – but only if sufficiently committed.

Gooch's success during 1990 bolstered not only his self-confidence. Mike Denness, the last England captain to have won a Test against the West Indies, believed he 'built in' charisma to his introverted nature. He was forcing himself to undertake aspects of captaincy and public life to which he was not naturally suited. Dealing with the media and public speaking did not come easily to him. During Gooch's first year as England captain, Dexter, once a journalist himself, Stewart, who disliked a section of the press but still coped with them, and Peter Smith, the Test and County Cricket Board's media relations manager, all advised Gooch on how to deal with interviewers. Smith was particularly well placed to do so, having previously written on cricket for two tabloid newspapers: the *News of the World* and then the *Daily Mail*. 'We worked hard with Graham,' said Dexter. 'We tried to help him along by anticipating questions and responses.' They were aware how important a part of the captain's role this had become. Regardless of the efficacy of his advice, Dexter now thought that Gooch would not make again the kind of comments that led him to compare his captain-in-waiting to a wet fish. 'On that occasion he got it wrong,' said Dexter.

Otherwise, chairman and captain saw little of each other away from the cauldron of Test cricket. 'Neither of us is particularly outgoing or chatty, so we stick to the essentials,' said Dexter, who preferred, anyway, to keep his distance. They would speak occasionally on the telephone as the summer of 1990 got under way. Most of Gooch's day-to-day dealings would be with Stewart, who watched more county cricket and who was more closely in touch with the England assessors.

Gooch's initial first-class match of the season was against Gatting and Middlesex, who were likely to be strong challengers for the championship. In a drawn match Gooch made 137 and 39, in both innings being caught at the wicket off Neil Williams, a bowler whom he rated highly. It was no coincidence that Williams played for England during the summer. Gooch followed this by making 215 with twenty-eight fours and a six against Leicestershire at Chelmsford, putting on a record 403 with Paul Prichard for the second wicket. Essex made 761 for 6, the highest score in their history. It was already clear that the balance between bat and ball, which had greatly favoured bowlers the previous season, had now swung too far in the other direction. The balls had been changed, the pitches had improved.

Gooch continued in this imperious vein. The touring Zimbabweans were next. Even though he held himself back in the Essex order – other captains in such form might well not have bothered playing – he still made a century coming in at number six. He did stand down from his county's match against Cambridge University before making his third championship century in four innings against Worcestershire, the champions. He was making runs, too, in one-day cricket: another century came off Nottinghamshire, and an unbeaten 94 against Northamptonshire enabled Essex to reach the Benson & Hedges quarter-finals. In spite of another good score (87), also against Nottinghamshire, they progressed no farther. In the two matches Essex played before elimination from the NatWest Trophy, Gooch made two further centuries, against Scotland and Hampshire, the latter of which was his eleventh of the summer in all cricket.

All this amounted to astonishingly consistent batting. Indeed, in the eleven first-class matches he played for Essex Gooch never scored less than a half-century. 'These were performances of great conscientiousness and of the highest order,' said Peter Roebuck. 'He is a superb professional cricketer.' Gower thought he was concentrating increasingly on his technique. 'He was trying to get his bat to come through straighter to stop him falling away. He calls it "the delivery of the bat". He had been working on this in 1989 but hadn't found the solution.' Gooch had in mind that in the first series of the summer he would be opening against a bowler he rated more highly than Terry Alderman: Sir Richard Hadlee. When asked to name the best bowler he has ever faced, as he often is, his answer is that Hadlee had no peer.

There were two one-day internationals against New Zealand in May, and still more runs for Gooch. He made 55 and an unbeaten 112 which effectively ensured England won the Texaco Trophy on run rate. His bowling, which at least one England coach thought was underutilised in one-day cricket, brought him useful wickets. Alan Knott reasoned that if he bowled himself more regularly he would become quicker. Gooch, though, had long been influenced by Fletcher's belief that his batting was of prime importance to his side and, as an opener, that he should never risk being over-tired.

Gooch felt now that he was batting as well as he had done for many years. Before the first Test he made another century for Essex, this against Middlesex at Ilford, following a duck in the first innings. The Test was to be at Trent Bridge, Hadlee's old ground. He was to play, in spite of a hand injury not dissimilar to Gooch's, the intention being that he would bowl but bat well down the order. England chose one player who had not been to the West Indies, Neil Fairbrother, which Gooch felt vindicated his assertion that it was not harder to get into the team than to get out – which was certainly once the case.

For individual feats, the rain-affected drawn match will best be remembered for Mike Atherton's 151, an innings which enabled England to recover from the parlous position of 45 for 3. What would have lingered longer in the memory for some was Hadlee's first ball of the series. It struck Gooch on the pad, on or around leg stump. His initial reaction was that it was going down the leg side, but, as with one or two umpiring decisions that were given in favour of the Australians the previous summer, so this appeal was upheld.

This provoked the inevitable comparisons with Gooch's problems against Alderman. His preference for faster, in-slant bowlers, with the ball coming on to the bat, was well documented. And not only did he not plant his left foot far down the pitch; he did not move his feet a great deal at all early in his innings. Any concerns,

though, that Hadlee would dismiss him cheaply throughout the series were dispelled in the second Test at Lord's.
There Gooch made 85 after England had been put in. It
was to be the top score in their innings. Hadlee had just
been honoured by the Queen, and Gooch remarked to
Atherton on their way out to bat that he had no intention
of becoming the first batsman to be dismissed by a
knight. He was not. He had struck twelve fours when he
tried to drive the off-spinner, John Bracewell, back over
his head and was caught and bowled. There have been
times when Gooch has appeared to get out to spinners
through not finding them as challenging as quicker
bowlers.

This match was also rain-affected. New Zealand had
the better of it, taking a first-innings lead of 128 through
a century by Trevor Franklin, 98 by John Wright and 86
off eighty-four balls by Hadlee in his last innings at
Lord's. Hadlee did dismiss Gooch in England's second
innings, knocking out his off stump when he had made
37, but with less than a day remaining a draw was the
inevitable outcome.

Between the second and third Tests, Essex played the
New Zealanders at Chelmsford. For this, their second
match of the summer against a touring team, Gooch
chose to open. He also chose to make a century – the
Essex supporters had come to expect nothing less – before
retiring with a jarred knee. He had by now been made
captain for England's series against India: if any appointment could be said to be a formality, this was it. First,
though, the series against New Zealand had to be settled
in the final Test at Edgbaston.

For a third time, Wright won the toss. He put England
in, admitting later he had made the wrong decision since
the pitch played well enough for Gooch and Atherton to

make 170 for the first wicket. Gooch had had so many opening partners since Geoff Boycott's Test career ended in 1981 that he himself once failed to spot on 'A Question of Sport' that the common factor between a motley group of batsmen was that they had all opened with him! In Atherton he had a partner who would seemingly be batting with him for the foreseeable future. 'You seem to get more strength batting with Graham,' said Atherton. 'He doesn't say a lot, but his determination and concentration are incredible. You find yourself thinking: If he can do it at his age, I've got to stick with him.'

Having been annoyed with himself for not reaching a century at Lord's, Gooch was determined, upon achieving 95 on the first day, to make a telling score on this occasion. He did. He reached 1,000 runs for the season, became the eleventh England batsman to make 5,000 Test runs and next morning achieved his ninth Test century. In all he made 154 off 281 balls. It was a match-winning performance. Indeed, other than Atherton's innings of 82 and 70, it was England's one decent score. Eddie Hemmings took six wickets in bowling out New Zealand for 249, whereupon England were unable to make as many quick runs as they would have liked. Gooch contributed 30 to a total of 158, which left their opponents needing 345 for victory. New Zealand fell well short, Malcolm taking five wickets.

There was no let-up in the hectic schedule of international cricket. Essex saw their captain for just two limited-overs matches before the next round of one-day internationals against India. He had not played against them in Test cricket for almost a decade; not, in fact, since the South African Breweries tour had been hatched. They brought now their quota of spinners and were not shy of playing them in the Texaco Trophy matches, where they found immediate success. India won the first of two with some ease through bowling out England for 229, of which Gooch made 45 before he was caught and bowled by Ravi Shastri. In the second, which India won by five wickets, Gooch lost his off stump shouldering arms before he had his eye in. For him, it was a rare aberration: usually he knows exactly where his stumps are.

Meantime, Essex were making considerable progress in the championship, having uncharacteristically been nearer the foot of the table than the top. They gained their third successive championship victory in the week of the first Test, the week of Gooch's thirty-seventh birthday. Lancashire set them 348 to win off a minimum of fifty-four overs, which they achieved with an over to spare. Gooch made 177, including twenty-one fours, from 152 balls.

In one respect, this was ideal preparation for the first Test of a new series. To say that Gooch was in form was an understatement. He was making runs off slow bowlers to boot. Atherton was not as guileful as the Indian leg-spinners, but it was greatly to Gooch's benefit that he bowled fourteen overs for Lancashire on the final afternoon. They were expensive.

For those opposed to Gooch's regimen of fitness and practice, there was seemingly conclusive evidence now that this was worthwhile. The match against Lancashire had been played in excessive heat. Two days later Gooch was batting again in similarly stifling weather, England having been put in by India at Lord's. In the West Indies he had made his name as a captain. According to *The Times*, in this match he attained greatness as a batsman. He will be remembered for ever for his innings of 333, exemplary for his skill and bearing. He was exhausted at the end of the first day – the upshot, he thought, of his endeavours against Lancashire. His adherence to fitness enabled him to bat as thrillingly on the following day, for triple centuries are normally the preserve of far younger men. This was the astonishing aspect of his innings, the sixth-highest in Test cricket. 'I was not tired at the end,' he said. 'My reactions are slowed, my arms tire – but that is why I train.'

In that England innings records aplenty were broken, to the mortification of India's wicket-keeper, Kiran More, who dropped a comparatively straightforward chance when Gooch had made no more than 36. Gooch and Allan Lamb put on 308, the highest partnership for England against India; Gooch's innings of 627 minutes, which included forty-three fours and three sixes, was the highest score at Lord's, the third-highest by an England batsman, being thirty-one short of Sir Leonard Hutton's record 364 and only thirty-two runs short of Sir Gary Sobers's world-record unbeaten 365. Had he set his mind upon surpassing that, Gooch would probably have done so. As ever, he was aware of his team's needs, that they had to give themselves time to bowl out India. Although he has a sketchy knowledge of cricket history, he was aware that the record was within his compass; but more acutely so after he was out, when it dawned on him that he would most probably never come close to such a feat again. 'Most cricketers don't get the chance to bat that long,' he said. 'I was excited inwardly but don't show my emotions.'

The *Sunday Times* was baffled by his demeanour to the extent of labelling him 'possibly the most lugubrious sportsman in history'. This was coined after Gooch's own description of the moment when he reached his triple century: 'The first ball after tea, however, brought relief when I glanced Shastri for a single.' Likewise, there were no garrulous quotes from Brenda – 'Graham is not like Essex Man, he does not get ecstatic' – who did not see that particular moment owing to the BBC having made an untimely switch to racing at Ascot.

The only first-class cricket Alf had seen before he watched his son was when Hutton made his great score of 364 at the Oval in 1938 – not that he can recall anything about it. Hutton himself was at Lord's to watch Gooch. He died only a few weeks later, having seen that his achievement would stand, quite possibly for ever. He described Gooch as a good, rather than a great batsman. Others were more effusive, including Dexter. 'The way he plays and moves, I thought he could not be a good player of spin. Yet he is the best batsman against spinners I have ever seen. His potential weakness is that he finds it so easy he thinks everyone else will, too.'

That Test, Gooch reckoned, was the finest he has played in. Almost overlooked amid the welter of runs was the small matter of his century in the second innings. His 123 off 113 balls beat Greg Chappell's aggregate record for a Test by seventy-six runs. With Atherton he put on 204, a record partnership for England's first wicket against India. All this and centuries from Shastri and Mohammad Azharuddin, atoning for his decision to put England in, as well as some vast hitting by Kapil Dev. Fittingly, Gooch was responsible for India losing their last second-innings wicket and consequently the match, running out their last batsman through a swoop, pick-up and direct hit from mid-on that would have pleased a fielder half his age. There was no disputing the man of the match, Gooch's match, the abiding memory of which is him moving down the pitch to smite another flighted delivery to some remote corner of Lord's.

Needless to say, the Turbo bat he was wielding received much publicity. Manufacturing had changed since he was a boy in that a bat would sell as a result of the model rather than a player's name emblazoned on the face. Even so, he personally signed 3 lb 'Turbo Test Selection' bats for Stuart Surridge. He had come up with the name, just as he had with 'Box Briefs'. His success, of course, was of inestimable value to the firm. 'Shops had to buy the products as he was England captain,' said 'Tiger' Surridge.

No man who scores 456 runs in a Test match can expect much privacy thereafter. 'If Ian Botham, the people's hero, had achieved such a feat, there would have been instant demands for a knighthood and Botham would have savoured the attention,' wrote Alan Lee. 'Gooch is different. More like a natter with his devoted parents, a pint of proper beer and a night in with the kids.' The day after the Test he presented a cheque for the largest Littlewoods Pools payout. There was a photograph of him standing next to a board that announced 'Last player retired rich'. It was symbolic: in time he surely would, too.

He felt no sense of anticlimax when he returned to Essex for Southend week. The square at Southchurch Park was now under the supervision of the county's groundsman, who allayed any concern that they would be penalised again. Gooch batted with a freedom not shown by any other batsman in making 87 and an unbeaten 65 that led to a ten-wicket victory over Nottinghamshire. Alas for Essex, just as they were making an impression in the championship they lost their captain again to England.

In the second Test against India, Gooch broke yet another record. In making 116 he became the first English batsman for nineteen years to score centuries in three successive Test innings. There was a further glut of centuries in this drawn match – six in all. For once, Gooch did not play the outstanding innings, the limelight being stolen by the seventeen-year-old Sachin Tendulkar, whose second-innings century enabled India to draw when they seemed doomed.

The one surprise in this match was that Gooch made only 7 in his second innings. It mattered little in that there were abundant runs forthcoming from several others. Back on the county circuit he made 9 and 53 in another comprehensive Essex victory, this against Surrey. There was one last Test against India and still more records to fall: in another high-scoring draw Gooch took further runs off what had come to be seen as an ordinary attack. But, as he said wryly, that was not his fault. He was there to take advantage of it.

First, he lost the toss for the fifth time in six Tests. Two centuries by Shastri and Kapil Dev helped India to reach 606 for 9; one by Gower on the final day brought the tally of centuries to fifteen, a record for a three-match series. Gooch's contributions, 85 and 88, meant that he overtook Zaheer Abbas's record aggregate of 583 runs in a three-match series and Sir Donald Bradman's 974 runs in an English summer. He finished with 1,058 runs from the two series, having had four more innings than Bradman. Typically, he regarded this as of secondary importance. He was more concerned that England had not lost the match.

There was now, of course, great kudos to be had from taking Gooch's wicket. In the next match the England captain played, for Essex at Northampton, he survived a strong appeal from Winston Davis, the West Indian fast bowler, in the very first over. This was turned down by the umpire, Kevin Lyons, which did not please Davis. He stood sulking in the middle of the pitch, returning to his mark only when the umpire motioned to Allan Lamb, Northamptonshire's captain, to have a word with him. Davis was subsequently fined and left the club at the end of the season.

Such behaviour only results in motivating Gooch, as do taunts from fast bowlers. He can give as good as he gets, just as his father has a short answer for those who are critical of him: 'Take a look at the scorebooks.' Gooch's score that day was 174, including a six and thirty-one fours, and in the second innings 126, his twelfth first-class century of the season. He and John Stephenson became only the third pair to make a double-century opening partnership in each innings of a first-class match. There were 1,285 runs scored altogether, too many for a three-day match to result in anything other than a draw. In the return encounter at Chelmsford a few days later, Northamptonshire beat Essex by 276 runs, a result which meant that Essex would be most unlikely to win the championship. There were yet more runs for Gooch, 92 and 40, but a second-innings glut from North-amptonshire's batsmen proved decisive.

Essex drew both their last two fixtures, with Kent and Surrey. At the start of their punultimate match, Gooch needed 254 runs to become the first batsman since Bill Alley in 1961 to score 3,000 in a season. Given his remark-able consistency he would almost certainly have achieved this had he not broken a thumb in two places attempting to catch Trevor Ward on the first morning of the match against Kent. By now he knew all about hand injuries (and it was not to be his last of the year) but he was confident that he would be fully fit for the start of the tour of Australia that winter. Disappointment at this

injury and, for the second year running, narrowly failing
to win the championship, was tempered by his achievements of the summer.

Even so, Gooch's head was not turned. He was all too
aware that there had been an unfair balance between bat
and ball and was embarrassed to be mentioned in the
same breath as Sobers and Hutton, yet with a score of
333, a championship average of 99 and a first-class average of 101 comparisons would inevitably be made.
Wisden, the ultimate arbiter, was to headline its assessment 'A Genuinely Great Cricketer'. Ray East, who
departed Essex at the end of that season, was especially
impressed with the example he had set young people.
'Graham has been magnificent for young people to follow
– there is not a better professional cricketer in the world.
Most people would like him to show some more
expression, but he deserves his success. You do if you're
prepared to run to the ground from home!'

Gooch, his broken thumb strapped up, travelled to the
Oval for his county's final match of the season. He gave
Jonathan Lewis, whose début it was, champagne for scoring a century – joking that it was on the proviso he did
not turn out like Lilley, who had also scored a century
in his first match for Essex. With that he took himself
off to Toronto for two one-day exhibition matches on
artificial pitches against the West Indies. He had agreed
to captain an England eleven before he broke his thumb:
there was an attraction also in that he was able to take
Brenda and the children, who in turn were attracted by
the prospect of a visit to Disney World. The Test and
County Cricket Board had disapproved of the venture,
yet the players were not then under contract to the Board.

The England eleven lost both matches – not that anyone particularly cared. Sitting in the baseball dugout at

A 'wet fish' no more. Ted Dexter justifying to the media his appointment of Gooch as England captain in September 1989 *(The Times)*

The sweet taste of victory. Robin Smith, Graham Gooch, Devon Malcolm and Allan Lamb take a rare day off after defeating West Indies in Jamaica, 1990 *(Graham Morris)*

On the road to greatness. Sweat, guts and grim defence during England's first Test victory over West Indies for sixteen years *(AP)*

Turning point in the Caribbean. Gooch, his hand broken in Trinidad, is helped off the field by Richie Richardson and physio Laurie Brown *(Graham Morris)*

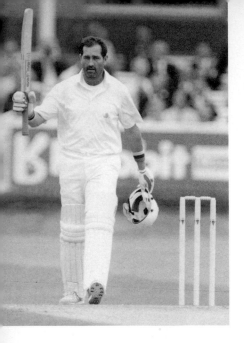

Left Gooch raises his bat after reaching his first century against India at Lord's in 1990. He continued until he had made 333 *(Adrian Murrell/Allsport)*

Below Gooch musing over his record 333 the day after the Lord's Test at a presentation ceremony to a Littlewoods pools winner *(The Times)*

Above   Adelaide, 1991. Gooch on his way to his first century in Australia, watched by Ian Healy *(Graham Morris)*

Right   Gooch displaying his OBE with Brenda and Hannah outside Buckingham Palace after returning from Australia. The glum faces may be on account of Brenda dropping the award in the gravel *(Universal Pictorial Press)*

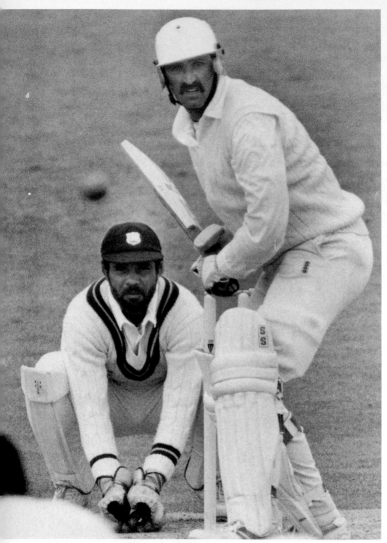

His finest innings. Gooch, ever vigilant during his unbeaten 154 at Headingley, is watched by an old adversary, Jeff Dujon (*Chris Smith/Sunday Times*)

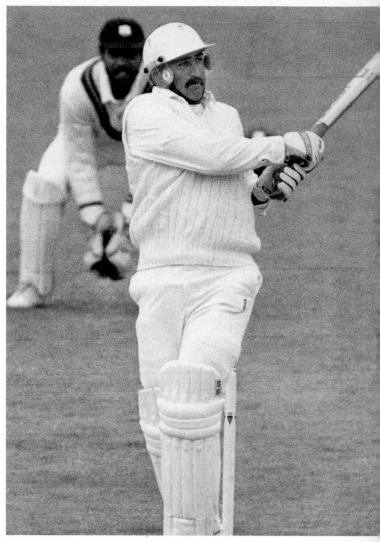

The late flowering: Gooch counter-attacking against West Indies during 1991 *(Chris Smith/Sunday Times)*

Left Trudging away from the wicket after being dismissed for 133 in the unlikeliest way – after handling the ball – in the second innings of the Old Trafford Test against Australia, June 1993 *(David Giles/PA)*

Below Down and out: a pensive Gooch, supported by the TCCB press officer Ken Lawrence, explains to the assembled journalists why he has resigned the England captaincy *(Adrian Murrell /Allsport)*

the Exhibition Stadium, Gooch mused that, had he been born in the United States, the dugout might well have been his permanent pavilion – in which case he would be earning a baseball salary of three or four million dollars a year. Then, he said, he would be more co-operative with the press. Never one to believe in the symbiosis of professional sport and the media, he found he was having to live with the fact that even in the States his time was as vital to others as it was to him. 'Everyone in the streets walks up to you. You can't disappear into a corner without someone bothering you. That's the price you pay. It used to happen quite a lot. Now it's every time.'

10

Frustration and Fury

Six years after Gooch had been outlawed from international cricket and two years after he had been on the
brink of fulfilling his contract with Western Province, he
was perceived in England not only as a sporting hero but
also as a true patriot. It was like Churchill changing parties. Indeed, he was patriotic: Essex was still his first love
but, if he had not had special affinity with the England
team hitherto, he certainly had one now. He had no hesitation when Dexter asked him to lead England to Australia. He was as thrilled as he can ever appear to be. This
was the summit of his career.

In terms of selection of a team or a touring party,
Gooch had more say than has any England captain prior
to Dexter's appointment as chairman of the England committee. On the selection subcommittee, the captain now
had one vote in three (the others belonging to the chairman and the manager) rather than one vote in five, as
was the case with the old system of selection. Gooch did
not necessarily have the final say since Dexter made it
clear that he wanted meetings conducted as he saw fit.
Gooch expressed his views clearly, was a champion of
youth in spite of his own age and was keen only to have
players who would push themselves in Australia. He
believed strongly in not overprotecting players. He him-

self had been chosen for England at a young age and he felt that selections as often as not tended to err on the side of experience. He did want Wayne Larkins, then almost thirty-seven, in the party for Australia; equally he was prepared to be persuaded by John Emburey, whose judgement he respected more than that of anyone else, that Phil Tufnell, who was twenty-four, was the best spin bowler in the country and should also be included – and Gooch had been impressed on the occasions he had batted against him. The idea, though, that the selectors can wave a wand and come up with a new magic formula is illusory: of most England tour parties the majority will pick themselves. On this occasion the selection meeting did not last long.

Upon returning from Disney World, Gooch had the plaster taken off his broken thumb and was soon outpacing players ten and fifteen years younger than him at the National Sports Centre, Lilleshall. His adherence to fitness, the importance of which had been drummed into him by Brian Taylor all those years ago, was matched only by his meticulous care for his kit. In that, he had been disciplined by his other county captain, Keith Fletcher. 'Look after your equipment,' Fletcher would tell him. 'They are the tools of your trade. If you don't look after them, you cannot do the job properly.' He was also influenced by Geoff Boycott's assiduous preparation.

In addition to his Turbo bats, Gooch's cricket bag would contain three or four left-hand gloves to every right-hand glove. This was because he was especially strong in his top hand and hence sweated more in that glove. Even for a tournament as short as a World Cup, he would take with him around nine gloves. They would be numbered, a sign of his fussiness and, perhaps, insecurity. Superstition dictated that he changed his right-hand glove when he reached a half-century, and he would start each new session with a clean dry pair. All in all he was inordinately concerned with comfort and the exact fit of his equipment. At one time he would sew the top knuckles of his gloves together as a precaution against a broken finger: blows on the hands were inevitable for any batsman, especially an opener. He put extra protection in his pads and fussed around with the straps. Box Briefs, chest protector (against the West Indies), thigh pad, white helmet, arm protector, cap, floppy sun-hat, sweatbands, T-shirts for batting in the nets, rubber grips for his bats – there was no end to the equipment. He would be generous with surplus gear he was sent by other manufacturers in that he would give it away to Essex players who otherwise would not receive such riches.

On the eve of departure for Australia, Gooch was asked to report to the party's Heathrow hotel earlier than was normally the case. He protested, but for all his suspicions was taken unawares when Michael Aspel produced his red book and pronounced: 'Graham Gooch, this is your life!' Even then, Gooch's face showed barely a flicker of emotion. 'Oh dear!' he said. 'Carry on.' In addition to appearances from numerous well-known cricketers, his mother reminded him that she pushed him round many a boundary in his carry-cot while his father was at the crease. Alf told of standing him on an attaché case with screw-in legs so that he could see West Ham play from the terraces at Upton Park. Douglas Kemp, his old schoolmaster, came on to say he had been certain Gooch would turn out to be a good leader. Graham Hammond, his best schoolfriend, also appeared. Geoff Boycott was especially generous, proclaiming: 'It was a great pleasure and a privilege to bat with him. He's a great pro.' Boycott looked ominously all set for one of his marathon innings.

There was a second farewell to the children and Brenda, who just about managed to stem the tears.

England flew to Perth the next day. There, they were to acclimatise and play their opening matches. There was also plenty of net practice. It was only five weeks since Gooch had fractured his left thumb; now he had just started to bowl in the nets at Robin Smith when a fierce return drive split the ring finger on his right hand, causing a gash so deep between the two joints that bone could be seen. The good news was that there was no break. Having not missed a match through injury for seventeen years, Gooch had now suffered three hand injuries in seven months. He was to have missed the opening three matches but was allowed to play solely as a batsman against a Country eleven at Geraldton, where he made 10 and 47. Against Western Australia, Gooch would have to field or not play at all. He kept himself away from the slips on the first day. In experimenting with fielding there later in the match, he dropped a relatively straightforward catch, which inevitably affected his confidence.

The match was a harbinger of what was to come. England did not perform well, just managing to draw. Worse, Gooch was to be troubled further by his finger. Before their match against South Australia he started to suffer pain to the extent of not being able to catch the ball in fielding practice. The finger had evidently become infected before the wound had healed. A hand specialist, Randall Sach, informed Gooch that it was poisoned and that he must have an immediate operation to drain the pus. This would mean missing the first Test; the alternative would mean missing a finger or a hand – permanently.

Had the specialist not been found, or if he had opted to start eating the dinner that had just been laid in front of him, Gooch's career would almost certainly have ended. What then? Gone overnight would be the sponsorships, the glamour, the trimmings. There would be work from Stuart Surridge, some speaking engagements, a decent pension (through his own initiative) – and a considerable drop in income. Gooch's insecurity, his keenness to make as much money from his chosen profession as he could while he could – this was suddenly comprehensible to all and sundry.

Once again Gooch would have to hand over the captaincy to Lamb. Once again there would be a severe test of the leadership capabilities of a man whose sociability, counterpointing his captain's introspection, was considered his one notable asset for captaincy. Again Gooch would have to evaluate whether he would be an unwelcome intruder at the vice-captain's feast. He did not seriously consider returning home and had his stitches removed the day before the first Test in Brisbane.

He was an anguished onlooker, as he was to be throughout the series in which England's cricket rarely gelled. Several of the players were out of form come the first Test, in marked contrast to Bruce Reid and Terry Alderman, who bowled superbly. All out for 194, England did manage to fight back well, gaining a first-innings lead of 42 through Angus Fraser, Gladstone Small and Chris Lewis, who took three wickets apiece. Then they lost their way. Dismissed for an abject 114, they were beaten by ten wickets within three days. Lamb took the blame – for England's batting failures rather than for his visit to a Gold Coast casino on the second night of the Test, fifty miles from Brisbane. He was in the company of Kerry Packer, Tony Greig and David Gower, who had at least made some runs in the first innings. Undoubtedly Gooch was let down, although with hindsight he was annoyed that the press had been so critical of Lamb when they would have had nothing but praise had he scored a century. In an age of less asperity and fewer reporters a Sobers or a Dexter, who like Lamb would not have appreciated curfews, might have done just that. Gooch had worked Lamb out for himself. He had appreciated his efforts in the Caribbean, counted him as a friend, but was aware of his weaknesses as well as his strengths. 'He knows all about him,' said David Norrie. And as the tour wore on he was to feel increasingly disappointed by the example both Lamb and Gower set to the younger players.

Lamb had now lost all three matches in which he had deputised for the captain. By contrast Gooch had led England ten times and lost only once, that in his first match against the West Indies. In those ten matches he not only had a batting average of 80 but had shown fierce resolve in ensuring that divisions, distractions and dissensions were a thing of England's past. The danger now was that his efforts might be in vain. The younger players had drawn inspiration from Gooch's example: for them he could not return soon enough. After a further defeat in the first of the Benson & Hedges one-day matches, Gooch, Stewart and Lamb thought the time had come to make their views known. They felt strongly that several individuals were not giving of their best.

Some months later, when Stewart had mulled over what had gone wrong on the tour, he concluded that there was a fundamental difference in the attitudes of the two nations. 'It is hard work getting what we want since a lot of people in Britain like cricket to be based on social life,' he said. 'That is because the peripheral side of the game is so pleasant. In a high-profile sport, sometimes the peripheral privileges come first with some players.

They find it hard to maintain the performances which got them there. In Britain there is a great deal of cricket. In Australia, if a person does not have the ability to be among the best in his area, then he will not be given a game. Hence the quality and standard is higher in Australia.'

Gooch was to make his feelings public in an interview he gave to Jon Agnew, who had retired from playing for Leicestershire and was working for *Today*. It can be easier for one first-class cricketer to speak to another in such circumstances, as was the case now. 'I thought it was strange that Graham felt inclined to attack the team,' said Peter Roebuck, who was covering the tour. 'He chose the players, therefore his judgement of players could be doubted.'

Realising that England's cricket appeared as inadequate from the dressing-room as it did in the middle, Gooch knew that, if at all possible, he must return earlier than planned. England were struggling in the Benson & Hedges matches; Lamb and Gower, the two senior players, were both suffering from ailments. He included himself at number five for the one-day match against a Bradman eleven at Bowral, Sir Donald's birthplace, making 7 in a match England also lost. Gooch did make some runs in two further Benson & Hedges matches, 48 and 41. His hand was still troubling him, the wound having opened up in the field, but he would be fit enough for the second Test, starting on Boxing Day.

The likelihood was that he would still be an influential figure in the series, in spite of his baffling record against Australia. Excluding his innings of 196 against them at the Oval in 1985 he averaged just 23. It was not good enough, and he knew it. He had proved on countless occasions he could play extreme pace and spin, but his natural method gave him less scope against what Keith Fletcher called 'dobbies'. In 1989, Terry Alderman had probed technical weaknesses to the point that Gooch's career could have been ended, either voluntarily or through his non-selection. Now Alderman and the like had to be faced again, and, what was more, England were desperately looking to their captain for a lead.

Power had changed Gooch as it had not changed Gower or Botham. The series was not yet lost, and he was determined there should be no spineless surrender. Not everyone appreciated having nets on Christmas Day morning, yet no one could be dissenting when the captain was himself barely ready for the fray and yet was a willing slave to training. Lamb was not fit, having run five miles back to his motel after making a three-hour century in England's previous match, against Victoria. 'It was a foolish decision, something which even the obsessively fit Gooch would surely not have done. His views on that incident are unspoken and, I suspect, unprintable,' said Alan Lee, who thought that if Gooch delayed his return any longer the tour might drift irretrievably out of control.

This was Gooch's first Christmas away from his children. It was as well for him the Test was starting on Boxing Day: there was much to fill his mind. Around 50,000 people were in the ground at Melbourne in spite of a new stand being built on one side of the ground. No sooner had Gooch won the toss and batted than he was out to the dreaded Alderman, leg before, padding-up. On a flat pitch there were runs from Larkins, who made a half-century, and Gower, who was in glorious form in spite of not being fully fit. His century enabled England to make 352, which they followed up by bowling out Australia for 306. Angus Fraser, whom Gooch greatly admired, bowled splendidly in spite of an ankle injury, having a spell of 6 for 23.

England began soundly enough in their second innings, although Mike Atherton was out cheaply again. Gooch, untroubled by his finger, batted capably enough in making 58; and Larkins, whose selection for the tour had been roundly criticised, managed another half-century. Thereupon England collapsed ignominiously. Larkins and Gooch scored 112 runs between them. The rest of the side plus extras managed just 38. Reid showed just how successful his recovery from a serious back injury had been by taking 7 for 51. Australia were left needing 197 to win and, although they lost two wickets before the close that evening, they won without further mishap the following afternoon.

By now, Dexter had arrived in Australia and had formed the opinion that England had played too much cricket in the year since their tour of the West Indies began. The schedule in Australia allowed for precious few days off. 'Graham was deeply upset,' said Dexter. 'He took it as a personal failure. The most important thing for him was that although things were going wrong there was no reason for other players to be saying, "We told you this would happen. If only we had had so-and-so . . ."' Gooch said retrospectively that he was never close to quitting the captaincy in Australia – 'that would have been copping out' – but at the time Norrie was not so sure. 'He was really hacked off at Melbourne. It was his lowest period as captain. He had been let down by Lamb going to the casino, a dreadful wicket at Brisbane and now this.'

Far from being criticised by the press for England's plight, Gooch was reckoned to have blamed himself for too much of what had gone wrong. He spoke of there being no magic wands, no easy options, and no substitute for hard work, and yet thought he had failed as captain. 'He was being driven to distraction by an impotent response which began with an unsuitable vice-captain and ended with a batting order which never allowed an innings to pass without spectacular collapse,' wrote Alan Lee in *The Times*. 'The chances are high that this will be the first England team to complete an Australian tour without a first-class win. While this may not be an unfair reflection on a dreadfully disappointing party, it would be an unjust endorsement on the licence of the captain. Could the time be near when Gooch may consider no job is worth this much heart-ache? And if he does, where on earth do England find a suitable replacement?' Indeed, of all the legacies of a barren tour, Gooch's loss would be the hardest for English cricket to bear.

Gooch was cheered up by the New Year's Honours list, in which he was awarded the OBE, and was able to laugh at an Australian broadcaster who said it stood for 'Overwhelmingly Beaten England'. Alas for him, that was the case again on New Year's Day when Australia won another contest in the long-running World Series Cup. England's chances of reaching the finals looked increasingly remote. The third Test, also played in Sydney, swiftly followed. If Gooch thought that the second Test in Melbourne had been bad enough, he was soon disillusioned again. Australia won the toss and made 518. The second day on which they batted, the Saturday, was described by Gooch as the worst cricketing day of his life. 'The previous Saturday had been bad enough when we surrendered the second Test but we lost our pride and dignity here at the SCG. The England cricket team had become a laughing-stock. Our poor bowling exposed our pathetic fielding. This was the worst fielding side I'd ever been in. It was a total disaster. I felt helpless, responsible and embarrassed. I would never have believed that any side I was in charge of could be so inept,' he wrote in *Testing Times*, his account of the tour. These were astonishingly strong words for any England captain, let alone one as reserved and diplomatic as Gooch. Hitherto England captains had not criticised players in public. Gooch's state of mind was not helped by a tantrum from Eddie Hemmings after an appeal for a catch at short leg off his own bowling had been turned down, and a display of petulance by Tufnell, who had already had his disagreements with umpire Peter McConnell in the second Test.

Ian Chappell, Australian captain turned commentator, said of Tufnell: 'The good thing is that when he's bowling he's not fielding.' The talented but zany spin bowler had finally taken his first Test wicket – to his credit his nerve had held after Dean Jones had made a calculated assault on his bowling earlier on the tour – only to turn his back on Gooch when congratulations were offered. Mike Selvey, another cricketer turned journalist, wrote in the *Guardian* that Tufnell was 'churlish'. He had been petulant in the nets, moaned that fielders were 'camels' and appeared to play up to the ''Ere we go' element in the crowd. 'Turning his back on Gooch was not a clever thing to do,' wrote Selvey. Gooch disliked virtually everything about Tufnell – his dress, his attitude, and particularly his attitude in Australia – and Tufnell thought he was being victimised. He misunderstood his captain: Gooch was not devious and would not have wasted his time plotting against an individual in his own side. The upshot was that although in public Gooch would confine himself to remarking euphemistically that Tufnell had to learn there was more to Test cricket than bowling, in reality Tufnell would do penance for his behaviour – even if there were times over the next few months, when, on sheer ability, he should have been chosen.

Of paramount importance now was that England make sufficient runs to give themselves a chance of victory, however remote that must have seemed. They had nothing to lose – an attitude personified by Gower. His century was still more spectacular than the one he scored at Melbourne. With Atherton making 105, Alec Stewart 91 and Gooch himself 59, England declared forty-nine runs behind, allowing them one hour plus the whole final day to try to win.

Australia had lost two wickets at the close of play on the fourth day, which gave Gooch reason to believe England could conceivably win. Australia did collapse to 166 for 7, at which point there were four hours still remaining. Bafflingly, Gooch chose now not to bowl Malcolm (who had been injured) at Carl Rackemann, a tail-ender who managed to block England's spinners for seventy-five balls without scoring a run. When Gooch did bring Malcolm on for his first over of the day, Rackemann was dismissed. Understandably, Gooch was widely criticised for tactical inflexibility (as he was for bowling Malcolm round the wicket at the left-handed Mark Taylor). England were ultimately left to make 255 in twenty-eight overs and, although Gooch and Gower struck 84 in twelve overs, Gooch making a rapid half-century in a desperate attempt not to concede the Ashes, the asking rate was impossible to maintain. England finished on 113 for 4.

Gooch had more to say, through the press. His dislike of dissent towards himself was matched by his antipathy to players who disagreed with umpiring decisions. In an article for the *News of the World* he suggested a 'sin-bin for cricket's bad boys'. He wrote: 'It's time umpires had more teeth. Why should they have to put up with so much aggro and abuse? If they could dish out instant retribution – a short, sharp punishment like sending off the offender – the trouble would soon stop. Umpires have no real power to enforce the laws. I was taught that when you're given out you go. I don't see why umpires should be abused. Controlling players is part of my job. But there's a limit. You tell them how you expect them to behave but you can't stop them if a fuse blows. I can't physically prevent players stepping out of line.'

There was another reason why he was finding captaincy more onerous than in the West Indies. This was because there was more to do and see in Australia, more diversions. The touring party did not necessarily mix together off the field. It was a fragmented group. In the very first week of the tour Gooch and Stewart had realised the atmosphere among the players was not what it had been in the West Indies but they seemed to be powerless to do anything about improving it.

Two days after the Sydney Test, England's last chance of winning a trophy on the tour disappeared when they failed to beat Australia in their final World Series qualifying match. Since he was unable to work out what was wrong with the players' attitudes, Gooch decided it would be best to contemplate alone. He let Lamb take the party to play New South Wales at Albury while he remained in Melbourne, watching tennis and golf. Significantly, Gower, whose advice Gooch had increasingly sought in the field, stationed himself in Sydney. He was a man apart and yet there was no one else other than Lamb of sufficient experience whom Gooch could rely on for support. Gooch denied, though, that he was becoming totally despondent. 'I had to live with whatever happened and be as optimistic as I could. I have learned a lot in the past few years and one good thing is to try and think positively no matter how bad everything seems.'

In Gooch's absence England lost to New South Wales. He rejoined them on the Gold Coast where England did gain their first victory. Gooch made 93, and there were centuries by Smith and John Morris as well as wickets taken by Tufnell. Yet this was overshadowed by a fly-past. The errant individuals saluting Smith's first century of the tour from two Tiger Moths were none other than Gower and Morris. Gooch was not amused. In fact he was furious, as furious as he can ever have been on a cricket field. The connection with Gower's Biggles garb at England's Christmas Day fancy-dress party had still to dawn when he discovered that Gower, whom he thought was back in the dressing-room, had returned to the air-field to pose for photographs. A disciplinary committee of Gooch, Stewart, tour manager Peter Lush and Lamb imposed a fine of £1,000 on both Gower and Morris. Gower felt this to be extremely severe: 'Graham was not as uncompromising as Mickey Stewart. What had occurred was more a disruption to the discipline they were trying to maintain. The incident appealed to Gra-ham's inner sense of humour if not to his outer sense. We had a tête-à-tête in Wellington later but there was nothing wrong with our friendship,' he said.

Had England been two–nil up in the series rather than vice versa, the incident might have been allowed to pass. No doubt the management was concerned about its public posture. Times had changed: it was two decades since an England captain had buzzed his players in a light aircraft while they were playing North Zone in a match in India. Tony Lewis was not disciplined then, and nor did he think Gower and Morris should be now. 'If anyone is in need of a laugh it is the England team. It is careworn, half-fit and unsuccessful. Now everyone can see what a grim cricket factory the England Test squad has become. It is a destroyer of talent and a squasher of the independent mind. Why is Graham Gooch so often seen yawning on the field? Because he is 37 years old and starts his tracksuit stint far too early in the day. He needs breakfast in bed occasionally. Volume of training, wall to wall practice has never been the answer to cricket,' he wrote in his *Sunday Telegraph* column.

They had to agree to disagree. It was no coincidence that Gower and Morris were not included in any England team the following summer and winter. As a result, Gooch received a bulging postbag from supporters of Gower, some of the letters anonymous, several of them vitriolic. He wrote back to all those who requested a reply (and submitted an address). Gooch was already questioning Gower's commitment in private and was to do so in public later in the year when asked directly during his public-speaking engagements. Gower admitted that it was hard to argue with Gooch's emphasis on training 'since he maintains what he wants to do'.

Would another captain have reacted as harshly as Gooch? Mike Gatting said he would not have liked the fact that Gower and Morris left the ground without permission. Gooch and Stewart had believed in loyalty to their players, but in return extra demands had been made on fitness and application, effort and discipline. Before the tour of the West Indies, Stewart and his coaches had spelled out their objectives. The results had been evident. Bobby Simpson, Australia's manager, was in accord with this. 'Graham's work ethic was just what was needed – when the team is struggling you have to work harder,' he said. Yet he had his criticisms. 'I don't think there was enough intensity in England's practice at times, but to get that everyone has to be a willing competitor.'

Gooch and Stewart now had to motivate an England party chastened by the diversion of the Carrara airshow. The Ashes would be retained by Australia, whatever happened, but the series could still be drawn. Alf and Rose arrived in Adelaide from London to watch their son: it was the first time they had seen him play Test cricket abroad. Gooch lost the toss and, even worse, his best bowler when Fraser was injured on the second day. Australia made 386 in their first innings, of which Mark Waugh, who refined his game playing for Essex, scored a century in his first Test innings. England's response was notable for Gooch's 87 – made out of 229 in nearly five hours – and the shot which brought about Gower's dismissal, a flick at a harmless delivery outside leg stump which was held at wide-ish long leg. It was the last ball before lunch, and England were already struggling. Gooch, batting at the other end, looked bewildered – and no one can look more bewildered than Gooch. Not comprehending the attitude of an individual who was the antithesis of himself, Gooch took an eternity to return to the pavilion for the lunch interval. When he reached it, he had nothing to say.

Even so, Gooch felt more let down by Gower's apparently insouciant attitude than by any one shot he played. Gower had, after all, scored two centuries already. There was seemingly no way out of this impasse for England other than to achieve a draw since Allan Border left them 482 to win in little more than a day. Gooch remained indomitable: he was still at the crease at lunchtime and determined to have an assault on the bowling. This he managed to the extent of scoring his first Test century in Australia, thirteen years and two tours after he first played there. His 117 came off 188 balls and included twelve fours. England could only draw – they had five wickets intact at the close – but Gooch had laid to rest any presumption that he could not score runs against Australia. Simpson felt the difference in his batting since 1989 could be attributed simply to his having sorted out his front-foot movement, though he admitted that Alderman was not as relentlessly probing as in 1989. 'Graham has to be appreciated as one of the best players of his era,' said Simpson.

The final Test was to be in Perth. Having won the toss for once, Gooch was bent on ensuring England made full use of a decent batting pitch. When they reached nearly 200 for the loss of only two wickets – Gooch had been caught behind off Craig McDermott for 13 – they really looked as if they were going to achieve a decent total. What happened then was that McDermott, whose Test career had been revitalised, took seven further wickets and England were dismissed for 244. 'I had never been in a side that had such a propensity to self-destruct,' admitted Gooch. Australia then made 307 on a pitch starting to show signs of wear. Gooch reckoned England needed to set their opponents around 250 to have any chance of winning, but once more their batting let them down badly. Again Gooch went to the new ball, this time making 18. He had run out of adjectives to describe England's cricket – indeed, he had run out of reasons for what had gone awry. After the Australians had completed a nine-wicket victory the next day, Gooch gave one last press conference. It was frank and damning.

'I have known only one way to play cricket and that is to compete in every game and every situation. At this level you have a right to assume that the players have the right attitude. One of my faults is that I am intolerant of players who are not putting in as much effort as I think they can. I suffer because I expect everyone to try as hard as I do. I also dislike playing on losing sides – it's not the way I was brought up. At the time you select who you think are the right personnel but you find out things about people as you go along. We all make mistakes. It's fair to say that a lot of players' careers will be on the line when we get back. Everyone has to look at their own performances honestly and decide whether they have given their best. It is my belief that some have not,' he said.

Of that touring party, Bicknell, Gower, Hemmings, Larkins, Morris and Small were not chosen for England for either the next series at home or their next tour abroad. Tufnell was only selected after serving time. County cricket was his gaol. Bicknell and Small struggled with injuries. Morris and Gower knew that they would have to excel for their counties before Gooch would contemplate having them in his side again.

That, of course, was on the assumption he would retain the England captaincy. After some misgivings he had stated his availability to continue in the role, if required. His concern was not so much that England had lost, as the manner in which this had happened. 'He is determined to win, but not at all costs, and as Essex are prepared to lose matches in order to win them he does not feel so much disappointment at losing as he would have done in the past,' said John Emburey, who kept in touch with him throughout the tour. 'But if a player is not committed Graham will give him short shrift.'

What made England's attitude the more surprising was that there was no doubting Gooch could lift other players through his own unwavering commitment and example, as opposed to his tactical acumen. He had no need of words when Malcolm or Tufnell misfielded, for he would dive and stop the ball himself. Jack Russell, ten years Gooch's junior and as dedicated a cricketer, admitted that he could not keep up with his captain in training, not after five fast laps of a ground and 200 sit-ups. 'Goochie is mentally so strong,' he said.

As for Gooch's opponents, they found he played the game in a hard but fair manner. And they liked him. From their perspective, Simpson described Gooch as 'quite a good captain' whose chances of success had been restricted by the performances of his bowlers and fielders. 'The thing that struck me was his frustration at his team's injuries and the difference he made when he returned after the first Test,' said Simpson.

Such criticism of Gooch almost invariably centred on his puritanical streak that resulted in lengthy practice sessions at the slightest opportunity. Peter Roebuck, who admired the way Gooch took responsibility for defeat, thought they were unproductive. Bob Willis, who commentated for Sky television, stuck up for Gower: 'Really gifted players don't conform. Part of their genius is their character being expressed.' He felt that there was a 'tunnel vision' approach to the tour: 'It was a case of "If you don't conform, you're not interested in playing". I was of the obsessive training school but not the obsessive practice school. Something had to be done to stiffen the resolve of the team but intensive coaching has not proved successful over the last two tours and England have been doing penance practice to keep the media and spectators on their side. You have to accept that the best practice facilities are not to be found on tour. Australia is the exception, but it is not the perfect place for building confidence.'

For all his disappointment, Gooch remained captivated

by cricket. England lost two of the three one-day matches in New Zealand that were tagged on to the end of the tour, a period which Gooch used to evaluate whether he still had something to offer as England captain. His conclusions that he had were in spite of his belief that he was never happier than when he was simply playing and practising. 'My motivation for being captain had nothing to do with the status – I didn't even think about that. I have noticed it now, of course. If I am out, people will nudge each other and point. People will want to talk to you when you are captain. You are in demand. There are others who relish all that, but I would rather go back to playing. The disappointing aspect of the tour was that Mickey and I could do nothing to change the atmosphere and it stayed exactly the same until the day we flew home. I don't think I endeared myself to the players by speaking my mind. On reflection, maybe I was harsh because nobody can give less than their best for England. But there were things which needed saying. I have searched my mind for reasons why it went wrong. We just didn't have the competitive edge we had in the West Indies. It baffles me. If I could have found out why, I would have put it right. I tried. I gave everything I had. I don't look in the mirror and think, "I should have done this. I should have done that." But I'm bitterly disappointed.'

11

Against the Odds

For Gooch, even more than for previous England captains, free time is at a premium. In part, this has been on account of the position having a higher profile than in the days of, say, Tony Lewis or Mike Denness two decades earlier. The media had proliferated, fanning public interest and awareness, 'Everybody wants Graham's time,' said Brenda. Her husband's message on the answering machine started: 'Once again, our team are all out. . . .' He is not slow to return calls. He has a car phone, a mobile phone, the use of a phone in the captain's room at Chelmsford: the telephone could have been invented for him. It takes him three hours every week to answer his letters – and those just the ones which request a reply or a signed photograph (which he always sends). As well as personal mail delivered to his home, up to fifty letters a week are sent to him via the Essex secretary/manager. Gooch opens them all himself, in his trophy-lined study or the captain's room at Chelmsford. He is inundated with demands from charities. 'I make a conscious effort to send memorabilia to everyone who sends letters,' he said. He is the figurehead for a branch of the Muscular Dystrophy Group of Great Britain and appears on their behalf to collect cheques. He does not publicise this. 'Graham is not one to milk publicity out of charity work,' said David Norrie. To deal with all this mail, Gooch had to enlist the help of Peter Edwards's assistants and his father. Fortunately, Alf has similar handwriting to his.

There is, of course, another reason why he has scant time to himself. He, more than most, was all too aware that the career of a cricketer, and especially an England captain, is finite. Equally he knew that during the life-span of an England captain there were commercial openings that would not come again. Gooch has his own accountant and solicitor to advise him (rather than going through his county club, as other Essex cricketers do) and had the benefit of Brenda's experience of book-keeping, but did not employ his own agent until Norrie began to look after his affairs in 1993. Hence he could be receptive to ideas from different sources. Agents such as Bagenal Harvey and Mike Newlyn have worked with him on projects ranging from talks at venues all round the country to personal appearances to ghost-written books. He found after-dinner speaking (which he hopes to continue after he retires) to be a lucrative pastime: in 1991 he spoke on four consecutive evenings in different parts of the country. Another day he spoke at a lunch in Bolton and a dinner in Blackpool. He liked to return home each night, even if the venue is as far north as Yorkshire, so his father would often chauffeur him and attend the dinner, too. 'Graham is a nightmare in the car,' said Alan Lilley. 'He switches the CD player on and falls asleep, or at least he did until he started taking vitamins.' Edwards, who has also ferried him round the country, soon came to the realisation that Gooch would be sleeping by the time it was his turn to drive. 'With others you might get annoyed but you accept he won't drive.' Edwards, a marketing man himself, admires the way

Gooch makes the most of his opportunities financially. 'We'd all like to do that,' he said.

Gooch's newspaper articles, like his books, are ghost-written. Norrie, who co-wrote *Testing Times*, also works with him on a syndicated local newspaper column. Then there is promotional work such as opening the Harrods 1991 sale with Viv Richards – Brenda was allowed to do some free shopping – and public relations for the holiday complex Dunas Douradas in Portugal, a country he likes and where he has bought a villa. He chooses to invest in property rather than in the stock market because that is what he knows about; and his friends emphasise his careful handling of money as well as his liking for it. 'He is very shrewd,' said Clive Radley. 'He thinks more about the financial rewards than most. He will be a long time not playing the game, and so it will be worth his while continuing for as long as possible since the financial rewards are so much greater now.'

The aspects of his life which became neglected after he was appointed England captain were gardening and DIY, which he enjoys. He did, though, manage to mend his roof on the same day that he gave a talk at the Brentwood Leisure Centre after the 1991 season. What he would not neglect, when he was still living with them, was his family. He has turned down numerous lucrative offers in order to be with them at weekends, when he might well take his children for a walk in a wood near his home. And he would often see members of his wider families.

'Graham has matured enormously since he gained the England captaincy and in so doing has become closer to people,' said Edwards. 'He couldn't have handled meeting the Queen and public speaking ten years ago,' said Lilley. 'He's more confident now.' Gooch himself knew that this was the key to standing up in public. 'You have to have confidence in what you are saying. People want to hear reminiscences.' So he tells them of the time in India when Ian Botham assured Keith Fletcher that every batsman would fall for his bouncer – India finished with a huge total – and when he discovered that Geoff Boycott's method of playing Richard Hadlee was from the non-striker's end. Such stories are always well received.

The only respite Gooch had pre-season was a family holiday in Portugal. He, Brenda and Hannah went to Buckingham Palace to receive his OBE, and he gained another award as Cornhill's England player of the year. He had of course been training rigorously. Brenda had given him a bicycle which he used increasingly to protect his knees from the pounding they were given through running on hard ground. He would cycle down the A12 to the county ground. He also did further weight training in his gym at home. He wanted to continue eating jam doughnuts almost as much as he wanted to extend his career.

Gooch met Dexter and Stewart to tell them he would be happy to continue as England captain and was duly appointed for the entire series against the West Indies. He still felt England had the talent to beat the finest team in the world, as they remained after overcoming Australia in the Caribbean. Pitting himself against the West Indies would again stretch him to the limit, and he would be thirty-eight during the summer, an age when many other cricketers favour a quieter life. The England cricket captaincy was perhaps the toughest role in sport, and here was Gooch prepared to give it another shot, eagerly rather than reluctantly. His enthusiasm had returned, although his message was no different from what it had been at the end of the tour of Australia. 'In every player there must be ability. But you don't need every player to be of the highest level of talent. We might need some-one who has less talent but has a great character, a strong character, a gritty fighter. This is true in an awful lot of sports,' he said.

Those were the stirring words that set the tone for what was to be expected in the new season. For Essex this began, as it so often does, in the Fens. Cambridge University were their opponents in weather so raw that an England captain recently returned from sunny climes could have been excused had he opted for the warmth of the pavilion. Not Gooch. Inevitably he played; equally inevitably he scored a century. As ever, Essex were expected to do well. The bookmakers rated their chances of success highly in all competitions. One individual, though, was not so taken with them. In a new book Graeme Hick, to whom the press were giving even more column inches than to Gooch, called them a team of moaners and suggested they were too used to success. Gooch did not pass comment on this (although he did have something to say about Hick's technique at the end of the summer). He was now the only player remaining from the county's first championship-winning side of 1979 and had under him an unusually young squad, bols-tered by Salim Malik, the Pakistani batsman, replacing Mark Waugh. Was it true that humour had gone from the dressing-room? Ray East, the greatest joker of them all, who had left the club the previous year, felt it was unfair to say that there was no fun under Gooch's leader-ship. 'Graham has a very pleasant sense of humour. I should know because he used to impersonate me! There is still laughter and harmony in the dressing-room,' he said.

The first weeks of the season were disrupted by cold and wet weather – and for Gooch a car crash. He had remained loyal to Toyota, who had long looked after him with sponsored cars and had just given him a brand-new model. The registration plate was H15 BAT, the idea being that this read like HIS BAT. It had replaced one ending in his initials, GAG, which he passed on to Alf for his car since he found it too ostentatious. He had given another plate ending in LBW to Brenda for her car. Having taken charge of this new Toyota, Gooch was (for once) driving Edwards, their destination not a dinner but a Sunday League match at Trent Bridge. Forced to brake at the top of a hill, Gooch's car was run into by Nasser Hussain, who was following. Hussain's car came off worst and had to be pushed to the side of the road. The Toyota made it to the ground, as did the two drivers, who managed to make the two highest scores in a match Essex lost.

For Gooch, as with most batsmen, the first few weeks of a dismal season were not prolific. Essex did reach the quarter-finals of the Benson & Hedges Cup through beating Middlesex, a match in which Gooch was out to Ricardo Ellcock, who was playing his first match since returning prematurely from the West Indies more than a year before. They won their quarter-final against Hampshire, not least through Gooch making a half-century. His one-day form was important to his country as well, for there was the customary round of one-day internationals against the West Indies.

As Viv Richards pointed out, Test cricket was still the real thing. He chose to make that observation after the three matches were over, each won by England. If nothing else, this was a fillip following events of the winter. In his first encounter with the West Indies since his injury on the 1990 tour, Gooch was bowled second ball by Curtly Ambrose. No matter: Ian Botham, returning to

England's side, took four wickets. In the second match at Old Trafford, Gooch made a half-century, putting on the 156 for the first wicket with Mike Atherton that led to England making their highest total in one-day cricket against the West Indies, 270 for 4. That proved beyond a side struggling with injuries. At Lord's a century by Neil Fairbrother, the first by an England batsman in home one-day internationals against West Indies, brought about a third victory. Gooch was out for 11.

At the end, the crowd having departed, a heated conversation could be espied from the press-box. On the dressing-room balcony Gooch was being harangued by Lamb as to why he was no longer England's vice-captain. He would not be placated by the explanation that he was not being demoted and that such an appointment would no longer be made. Lamb said publicly that he would not be available to lead England again. Doubtless Gooch was glad he had not reacted like that when initially passed over by Dexter.

With his reputation for honesty, Gooch was able to effect such changes: senior players like Gower and Lamb could not dissent for long with impunity. This also meant he could be ruthless in selection, whether for England or for Essex. There was no place for Gower when the squad for the first Test was announced: clearly there would not be until he had made some runs in county cricket.

The Test was to be at Headingley. Beforehand, Gooch spent some time at Geoff Boycott's house. They were still not close and, indeed, he felt Boycott made a meal out of the occasions he saw him – the temptation to take too much credit for coaching England had only just been avoided – but Gooch still had a high regard for his advice. 'Don't tell me Geoff couldn't play fast bowling,' he would say. Boycott's advice was invaluable. For once again the capacity of England's batsmen to withstand West Indies four-man pace attack would decide whether or not reduced odds of 9–2 against England winning were realistic.

There were reasons to believe they were. England's cosmopolitan side, including players of West Indian descent, had gained considerable confidence following their 3–0 victory in the Texaco Trophy matches. The West Indies lacked Ian Bishop and Gordon Greenidge, both of whom were injured. One had missed the tour in its entirety, the other had had to return home through a knee injury. This was the ground on which to win a Test, for often as not Headingley has yielded a positive result. Gooch by now was accustomed to Richards taking his time over making a decision upon winning the toss, as he did again. Indeed, Gooch was used to being kept waiting in the middle for as long as five minutes before Richards sauntered out to join him.

By the end of the first day, it was as if their last series in the Caribbean was still in continuance. England were put in and struggled. Gooch made 34, taking 12 off Malcolm Marshall's first five balls before the sixth reared at him, took the edge and was held by Jeff Dujon. Seven wickets had fallen for 174, and Gooch was sufficiently perturbed by his own relative failing to seek further advice from Boycott in the nets the following morning. Despite a half-century from Robin Smith and the doggedness of Mark Ramprakash, who in his first Test batted for 2½ hours in making 27, England mustered a seemingly friendly 198. But West Indies in their turn struggled to 173, restricted by nagging bowling backed up by astonishingly alert fielding: especially memorable were the agility and exuberance of Ramprakash and Gooch's sharp-witted running out of Richie Richardson.

England needed now to set a target of at least 250 in overcast conditions which continued to help seam bowling. When they were 38 for 3, and then 124 for 6, this looked far from likely. Gooch, though, remained, having survived an appeal for a catch at the wicket when 44. None of the fielders applauded when he reached 50, seemingly in protest (television replays appeared to show the ball hit his pad). Gooch's views on walking are absolute: 'If I know I have definitely hit the ball I walk off, although I do not get upset if other players don't. Ideally, I would like to go to the umpires before a match and tell them my players will wait for their decisions to make sure there is no misapprehension between the umpires and myself. For if a batsman does not walk for an obvious dismissal he cannot then make a fuss about a suspect decision.'

Thereafter, Gooch was rarely troubled in drawing the sting of the strongest attack in the game. Such was his relief that he began to play as if he were still the plundering batsman of yore. He himself felt he was not timing the ball in the middle of the bat – not initially, at any rate: few critics agreed. As he progressed from half-century to century, his concentration unswerving, his strokeplay commanding, it was apparent that this was one of the most valuable innings by an England captain this century. Derek Pringle was the vital partner Gooch needed, joining him when he had made 74. They were to add 98 for the seventh wicket. 'Since World War II no innings by an England captain has surpassed this,' wrote John Woodcock in *The Times*. 'It stands out not for artistic merit but for skill and courage against a very formidable attack in awkward conditions at a crucial time.'

On and on Gooch went. When he ran out of partners he had been batting for 7½ hours and had made an unbeaten 154. It was the first time he had ever carried his bat through a Test innings, and he was the first English player to do so in Test cricket since Boycott was left undefeated on 99 out of 215 against Australia in 1979–80. He scored far more than half England's total of 252 – 61.6 per cent, in fact, which was the highest proportion ever achieved by an England player. His name really could be put in lights, which was more than he himself would do. Gooch concurred that this was one of his finest innings and yet contented himself with a typical under-statement. 'I get great satisfaction scoring runs against West Indies,' he said. 'They have, after all, the best attack there is.' Among those who were more effusive was Dexter, who knew a thing or two about playing fast bowling himself. 'He is extraordinarily brave. I give him great credit for his late development and clearly his self-confidence has grown enormously. There is a link between captaincy and major scores. I had always felt that Gooch hit the ball too far in front of him. The best players I saw, Sobers, Viv Richards and Hutton, hit the ball under their bodies. At the top level players who have technical difficulties will be found out and Graham has had to modify the way he plays. He has technical frailties against pace bowling but can put his backlog of experience to good use,' said Dexter. According to the Coopers–Deloitte world ratings, which Dexter initiated, Gooch was now the best batsman in the world. That may not have been too far from the mark. In fifteen Tests as captain he had scored 2,004 runs at 74.22 as compared to an overall Test average of 43.20. No one else would have been quite so unmoved, outwardly at any rate, although Neil Foster was seeing a difference: 'Perhaps he became happier. He smiles more now. It is acknowledged what a good player he is, and human nature is such that he responds, just as he became very melancholy over his ban and press criticism for going to South Africa.'

Gooch's immediate concern, however, was winning the match. The West Indies, needing 273, lost one wicket on the fourth evening before capitulating by 115 runs on the final day. Unlike in Trinidad some sixteen months earlier, the weather was kind to England. This was their first victory over the West Indies in a home series since 1969, and hence the publicity was all the more extensive. Only a few months before, Gooch had been describing his England team as 'dreadful'. Now he was to say proudly: 'Beating the best side in the world proved English cricketers can still play a bit. And there's no reason why we can't do it again.' He added, as if conscious that a different kind of victory – the Gulf War – was being celebrated extravagantly in New York with 'the mother of all parades', 'the boys played well'. Dexter, who was by now of the opinion that the England players looked up to Gooch more than they had done to Mike Brearley, whom he felt was a lucky captain, described Gooch's unbeaten century as 'the most decisive innings to win a Test that I have seen'.

Such praise was still being handed down two days later as, grinning in embarrassment from ear to ear, Gooch was rapturously received at Chelmsford when he emerged for practice and then again when he went out to bat. Just occasionally Essex have the kind of day they had now, when their cricket reverts to amateurish habits. Put in by Worcestershire in their Benson & Hedges quarter-final, they were bowled out for 104. The match was over come mid-afternoon. As is the Essex way, such a débâcle does not lower spirits for long. A few days later they departed in high spirits for France, where they were to take on the national side in a match organised for David

East's Benefit by the Colchester wine merchants Lay & Wheeler. The fact that they were going to undertake a two-day tour of the champagne region doubtless had something to do with their jollity. For Gooch as with Pringle, the second Test was imminent and hence they were going just for the cricket.

The pitch was Astroturf on concrete in the grounds of Château Thoiry, where as many wolves as Frenchmen roamed. Just over the way from where the Sun King reigned at Versailles, the current monarch of English cricket took the first ball, and took it seriously. He had a score to settle. At Norlington School he had failed his French oral exam. Asked to describe what he could see out of the window, he thought he was being asked how many windows there were in the room and consequently failed. Now he made 34 off forty-six balls before he was caught Hafiz, bowled Shahzada. There followed a celebration in Urdu, the like of which will not be seen again until the International Cricket Council elect France to full Test status. Academic Gooch may not be, but undoubtedly through confidence derived from success he had become more conversant with language generally. His speech at a dinner that night, while not in French, was warmly received.

Gooch and Pringle returned to England and more serious matters on the first flight next morning. Lord's was their destination. Again Richards won the toss; again he deliberated long and hard before deciding to bat. A century by Carl Hooper enabled the West Indies to make 419 in their first innings, Pringle taking five wickets. England began poorly, losing their first three wickets for 16. Gooch, who took thirty-three balls to get off the mark, was missed on 13 and 35 before he was bowled, shouldering arms, by an extravagant breakback from

Walsh. His score of 37 was his lowest in a Test at Lord's as England captain. It took an undefeated century from Robin Smith and supportive innings from Pringle, Jack Russell and Phillip DeFreitas to ensure the follow-on was averted. Thenceforward rain spoiled the remainder of the match. England remained buoyant: Gooch resented being asked in an interview if rain suited England. His bullish view was that there was no point in playing if that was the attitude adopted.

The match became more memorable for Alf than for his son. Alf had asked him for a lift home on the last day, having planned to go to Lord's by train in the morning. There was a snag. Owing to rain, the England players were to meet the Queen not at the ground but at Buckingham Palace. Thus Gooch arrived with Alf in his car, to be told by the Queen's private secretary that only the team would be admitted to the state rooms. Gooch's concern for his father's well-being was such that the private secretary relented, ushering the pair into the state rooms where tea was served. They soon met the Queen. 'I said to Her Majesty, "This is a bit of a surprise – when I tell the wife she'll be livid,"' said Alf. 'The Queen chuckled. Had Rose come with me, I would not have met her.' Rose might not have made it to Buckingham Palace but she did at least sample some fruit cake, taken back to Gidea Park in a napkin by Alf.

Owing to Graham's fame, Alf and Rose were receiving other invitations. 'People have sought us out, but if I wasn't the father of the England captain they wouldn't want to know me,' said Alf. 'They get nothing out of me. Anyway, Graham doesn't tell us a thing about what he's doing, and I don't ask him – it's not our way. I don't know the reason why Gower is not in the England team.'

Alf and Rose continued to watch their son play all over

the country. While he was batting, Alf would not move. Together they went to Exmouth for a NatWest first-round tie in which Essex comfortably beat Devon. Gooch scored a half-century but has a more poignant memory: it was the last time he saw Leonard Hall, his first cricket master, who came to the ground in a wheelchair and died not long afterwards.

Essex now played Middlesex at Lord's, a match in which Gooch scored his eighty-sixth first-class century and also his thirteenth at headquarters, though statistics do not reveal that it came in a contrived way through joke bowling. Left to score 251 in a minimum of sixty-six overs, Middlesex were all out for 137. Foster was bowling beautifully, ensuring Essex kept abreast of Warwickshire at the top of the championship table. Banned from Test cricket as a result of playing in South Africa, he was leading the side when Gooch and Pringle were with England and felt Gooch valued his opinion when present. 'I discovered when I was in charge that the captain needs new ideas, and Derek and I are able to help Graham. Being captain of England made a huge difference to him at county level because it took away the pressure he had felt before when he led Essex. When someone bowls a bad ball the captain must not show frustration, and Graham does not drop his head too much now,' said Foster.

If his captaincy was considered to be improving all the while – not least by Mickey Stewart – Gooch remained platitudinous at press conferences. 'You hear me trot out the same things every time,' he said before the third Test at Trent Bridge. 'It doesn't change; it really doesn't. If we don't play well, we will get beaten. The West Indies are capable of coming back to win the series.' Not a truer word was said. On a good pitch England mustered 300, of which Gooch made 68, completing 2,000 runs against the West Indies in the process. The only other cricketers to have done so were Boycott and Sunil Gavaskar. Most batsmen would have been content with this, yet Gooch was concerned at being out for the second time in succession through not playing a shot. On this occasion he was lbw to Marshall.

The West Indies gained a first-innings lead of 97 through consistent batting down the order. They then took three quick wickets on Saturday evening, including that of Gooch, who was deceived by Ambrose's length and beaten on the back foot. He made 13. It was beginning to look as if supremacy in the series would be decided by the tussle between arguably the best batsman and the best fast bowler in the world. In spite of a late flurry the next day by DeFreitas and, improbably, Syd Lawrence, the West Indies were left needing only 115 to win, and this they achieved with only one wicket down. It seemed that even without Greenidge their greater individual ability was starting to tell.

The West Indies victory was overshadowed. The news that South Africa were to play international cricket again was welcomed by Gooch – he hoped to play against them before he retired – but he was surprised the ban imposed on those who took part in Mike Gatting's tour the previous year had not been lifted. He wrote to the Test and County Cricket Board reasoning that it should be, earning him the gratitude of Gatting. 'Graham asked that his letter be referred to the International Cricket Council, and it was very nice of him to write,' said Gatting. Naturally Gooch wanted the best England side possible, but he remembered how long it had taken him to get over his own ban, and his views on the rights of an individual to play where he wished had not changed. He was altogether astonished at the speed with which South Africa had returned to international cricket.

In the second round of the NatWest Trophy, Gooch made 95 in 146 balls against Sussex, an innings that won the tie for Essex and him the Man of the Match award. He followed this by equalling Greenidge's Sunday League record of eleven centuries and then making 97 off eighty-nine balls before lunch as Essex beat Somerset at South-end the following day. During that innings he felt the first symptoms of tonsillitis, which he had evidently caught off Brenda and the children, and which almost kept him out of the fourth Test; on the eve of the match he kept away from the other England players and took to his bed early. For all the speculation that he would miss the match (evidence, if it were needed, of his status and value to the side), Gooch was fit to play. Put in on an Edgbaston pitch of inconsistent bounce, England, without Smith, collapsed and were all out for 188. Gooch himself batted positively before lunch, making 45 before playing round a quick in-swinger from Marshall. The West Indies replied with 292, including a century by Richardson. Once again England made all too few runs in their second innings despite Gooch's 40 and a memorable ninth-wicket stand of 92 between Pringle and Chris Lewis that tantalisingly raised England's hopes. Needing 157 to take a 2–1 lead in the series, the West Indies lost three quick wickets before Richards and Hooper won the match with an increasingly assertive unbroken part-nership.

England's batting was betraying them. Lamb, Atherton and Hick had between them made 233 runs in twenty-three innings, and clearly there would have to be changes for the final Test. Before that Gooch met the Queen again when she opened the Ken Barrington Centre at the Oval (later she invited him once more to Buckingham Palace for lunch in November) on the day of Surrey's NatWest quarter-final against Essex. Gooch made his third half-century in three matches in this competition, and yet still Essex lost by 31 runs. He chose to go in at number six for his county against the West Indies, making 66 and an unbeaten 25 in a match that ended in a disappointing draw.

England's changes for the fifth Test at the Oval featured the return of Ian Botham and Smith after injury. Hick and Lamb were dropped, as was Russell, Gooch preferring Alec Stewart for his greater ability with the bat. There was also the post-penance return of Tufnell. The pitch was likely to take spin – and would also be the quickest of the series, as Gooch discovered for himself upon winning the toss and batting. The International Cricket Council had ruled that in future only one bouncer an over would be permissible in Test cricket. They had done so without consulting the likes of Gooch and Smith, England's two best players of quick bowling, who would have preferred the umpires to be given more authority. 'The game would not be better without bouncers,' said Gooch, 'but the umpires should enforce the law as it stands at the moment. By and large they don't.'

Gooch and Morris were now subjected to two bouncers an over as distinct from balls that lifted from just short of a length. They got those as well and coped admirably, putting on 112 for the first wicket, the best opening partnership of the series on either side. Gooch had made 60 when Ambrose had him lbw, cutting one back, and there was a collapse of the kind England knew all too well before another gutsy century by Smith enabled them to make a total of 419. Had Gooch not dropped a straight-forward catch in the slips in Botham's first over on his return to Test cricket, Desmond Haynes would not have made a half-century and Ladbroke's would have lost a great deal of money.

As it was, this scarcely mattered. For Tufnell showed just why he was regarded as the finest attacking spin bowler in the country, working his way through a West Indian order in which Richards came in at number eight owing to a migraine. Although Tufnell had been bowling consistently well in the championship, there had not been any pressure exerted upon Gooch from any member of the team who felt he should have been included earlier. The captain was omnipotent. Now, though, Tufnell took 6 for 25 as the West Indies collapsed in the manner of bygone days, bats whirling and heads panicking. They gave themselves little chance of averting the follow-on and, with Richards incapacitated and out cheaply, were dismissed when still 243 runs behind England.

For the first time since 1969 an England captain was in the luxurious position of being able to invite West Indies to follow on. And Gooch had no hesitation in issuing the invitation. The pitch was taking spin but did not look likely to deteriorate. If ever the West Indies could have been said to be there for the taking, this was the time. Again they were intent on attacking Tufnell – and they had more success. A century by Richardson, 60 in what was probably to be his last Test innings by Richards and a half-century by Hooper enabled them to reach 385, which left England needing 143 for victory. As a variation on the ritualistic huddle when England took the field on the final morning, Gooch stood at the pavilion gate and clapped each man encouragingly on the back. Only Botham was neglected: doubtless Gooch knew that he of all players, who had never played in an England side that had beaten the West Indies, had no need of that.

It would have been ideal for Gooch to have been at the wicket when the winning runs were scored. That, after all, had not happened in Jamaica. He made 29 now before going to Marshall. The lbw decision was marginal, as so often with one dismissed in this manner more frequently than most. None the less, England were not to be denied. After Stewart had thoroughly vindicated Gooch's judgement and Ramprakash had been out with the scores level, there was one last moment to savour in a magnificent match. 'It Ain't Over till the Fat Man Swings' was the *Guardian*'s headline, and indeed it was not. Botham sweetly dispatched his first ball for four and was engulfed by as big a crowd as had been seen on the last day of an Oval Test for many years.

The plaudits were heaped on Gooch. Dexter, whose job could be said to have been saved by his captain, called him 'a very special guy'. The same applied to Mickey Stewart, who named him England's Man of the Series. Lance Gibbs, West Indies manager, said of this citation: 'He deserves it not least for making this the happiest and most sporting of series I can remember.' Gooch himself reiterated his belief that his players could compete with any in the world even if, as usual, he did not give vent to his feelings.

'A friend rang me up and said Graham looked so miserable, England must have lost the Test,' said Brenda. In fact his success and his acceptance greatly pleased him. He was able to treat his jousting with the press as something of a game. 'If he didn't, he'd go crazy,' said Alan Lilley. 'He doesn't care what people think,' said Brenda. 'Sometimes I think: I wish he hadn't said that. But he's made his mark and, if people don't like it, that's unlucky.' Only those who were jealous of his achievements would not have liked it.

For much of the summer, Gooch's willingness to take part in the World Cup and to tour New Zealand, the one country where he had still to play Test cricket, had been in doubt. A few days after the end of the series against the West Indies, he put the England committee out of their misery. He laughed when Peter Edwards told him he could not really afford to go on tour, that he would make far more money from public speaking. Doubtless that was true. Yet he was enjoying being England captain. That he would remain so was a formality.

There was one last Test match that summer, against Sri Lanka at Lord's. There was, of course, the concern to Gooch that England might subconsciously relax against opponents who were not of the same standing as the West Indies. Since they were bowled out for 282 upon winning the toss there was the inference that they had. This was put to rights by dismissing Sri Lanka for 224, DeFreitas taking seven wickets, and being able to declare their second innings when only three wickets were down. One of these was Gooch's – but not before he had made 174, passing the achievements of others as he did so. The aggregate Test runs of two knights, Hutton and Bradman, was left in his wake. He became only the fifth England cricketer to make 7,000 runs in Test cricket. It was also his sixth Test century at Lord's, two more than anyone else in history; and, although one of the spinners, Anurasiri, was turning the ball appreciably out of the rough at one end, it would rank as one of his most untroubled.

At times, Gooch would step away outside leg stump and drive through extra cover. He would advance rhythmically to hit straight and even deployed the reverse sweep. There were nineteen fours in a 329-minute innings which ended when he charged down the pitch to drive

Anurasiri. 'His dismissal hinted at self-sacrifice, almost as if he had tired of belittling the bowlers,' wrote Alan Lee. With the help of further contributions from Smith and Stewart, Sri Lanka were left 423 to win, more than had been scored before to win a Test by a side batting last. That they did not make them owed much to Tufnell, who took five wickets as Sri Lanka were bowled out for 285.

Gooch had now made 2,000 Test runs in thirteen months, a remarkable achievement. His average was fractionally below those of Gower and Colin Cowdrey, two of the four England batsmen to have scored more runs than him at this level. Boycott, England's highest run-maker (8,114), was in Gooch's sights. The other batsman in this list, Wally Hammond, with an aggregate of 7,249, would doubtless soon be overtaken. The greater the success – both his and England's – the greater the spin-offs. First Artist, the agents who looked after both England's cricket and football teams, were receiving numerous telephone calls for possible endorsements from companies who had turned down their approaches after the tour of Australia.

Meanwhile Essex were making much headway in the championship. In Colchester week Gooch scored 173 against Northamptonshire, an innings which provided the ballast for a victory in two days. A further victory by an innings over Derbyshire, in which he scored 44, effectively meant that Warwickshire were their only rivals for the title. When, in their next match at Grace Road, Essex beat Leicestershire by nine wickets soon after lunch on the last day, they were kept waiting by Britannic Assurance in case Warwickshire failed to beat Northamptonshire. The championship and £44,000 would have been theirs. It transpired that they were delayed and frustrated, for Warwickshire ensured that nothing would be settled until the final four-day fixtures of the season. Fittingly, Essex, the prospective champions, were to play Middlesex, the reigning champions. If Essex won this match, Warwickshire could not overhaul them.

The first day proved conclusive. Often there is help for the new-ball bowlers in the opening overs at Chelmsford, although not to the extent that one side can expect to bowl out another for as little as 51. That was what happened now, Middlesex collapsing to record the lowest total of the season. Any concern, though, that the pitch would be reported was swiftly allayed by the way Essex batted. A flurry of drives mocked all that had gone before. They were made, inevitably, by Gooch. His sixth first-class century of the season was followed by his double century, reached in the final over of the day. The manner in which he did so paraphrased the cricket. Mike Gatting, the Middlesex captain, bowled a long hop, and Gooch swatted it for four. He had been batting for five hours and had given Essex a near-unassailable lead in the match and hence the championship.

There were no premature celebrations. Ten minutes after hurrying off the field with an undefeated 202 to his name, Gooch was sweeping out of the ground in his Toyota, fretting in case he be late for picking up Brenda for a shopping trip. The next morning he was in the Stuart Surridge factory at 7.30 for a photographic session before resuming his innings at Chelmsford. He finished with 259, the highest first-class score of the season, an innings that included two sixes and thirty-seven fours. When he was out, he plodded off unemotionally. Only when victory had been achieved did he forget himself, grabbing the microphone on the balcony and telling the crowd how emotional he felt. Anyone else and this would only have been expected. Coming from Gooch it was as unusual as was his revelation that 'this has definitely been the best year of my career'. He was drenched in champagne when he said this. Now a convert to four-day cricket, he admitted with some relief that 'finishing second three years on the trot would have been hard to take'. Even then, his ecstasy did not last. 'If I had not gone to the ground Graham would not have told me Essex had won the championship,' said Brenda.

It was the fifth time Essex had won the championship in thirteen seasons. The side had changed considerably. 'Graham is mellow, but the rest of us are fairly puerile and have tantrums,' said Foster. Gooch, thought Brenda, did not have much in common with those players in their early twenties. He could be severe, not least in his appraisal of Mike Garnham, the wicket-keeper. Yet he was swift to praise others, notably Foster: 'He has never bowled better. He is a class act.' In turn Foster felt that Gooch should have taken more of the credit for himself. Their success was praised thoroughly, for Essex were generally regarded as the best side in the championship. As a prize, if it could be so called, they were to play the winners of the Sheffield Shield, Victoria, at Chelmsford. Owing to the weather this was something of an anti-climax: Victoria won a one-day match (Gooch followed his double century with a duck), and the four-day match, in which he made 31 in his only innings, progressed to a dull draw lightened by a game of softball before play on the third morning to promote the World Corporate Games.

Gooch finished the season with a first-class average of 70. The word 'great' had been liberally, even automatically, applied to his batting for over a year now, and it had stuck. His captaincy, praised in more temperate language, was not so easily evaluated. The ultimate authoritative view belonged to Keith Fletcher. 'There were times when I wondered if Graham would ever be a leader, and I know he felt the same. But he has grown into it, improved tactically, learned man-management and developed a style and a love of the job. If anyone can take England back to the top in world cricket it is him. He is now very good indeed.'

The season, Gooch's season, had continued well into September, and yet his work had barely begun. As he looked ahead to an autumn of after-dinner speaking as well as twenty cricket talks around the country, lunch at Buckingham Palace (wearing shoes from Harrods), England practice sessions (sponsored, though the players were not paid), promotional work, television appearances, the Man of the Year lunch at the Hilton, meetings with solicitors, agents and accountants, negotiations over buying his property in the Algarve, a book launch and, most important of all, a family holiday abroad, it was clear just how far he had travelled in style, if not in distance, from his boyhood home. *The Times* summed up, not on their sports pages but in their leading feature article: 'Apotheosis of Essex Man.'

12

The Weary Victor

For all his varying commitments off the field before England left for New Zealand, Gooch missed only one (unpaid) training session in the autumn of 1991. He could be exonerated, for his alternative engagement was at Buckingham Palace: even Stewart's relentless regimen of work had to bow before a luncheon invitation from the Queen. Besides, Gooch remained as fit a cricketer as any in England's party. 'He has strength, endurance, a satisfactory cholesterol level – in fact, no weak areas,' said John Brewer, head of the Human Performance Centre at Lilleshall, after assessing all the players. 'Chris Lewis, Dermot Reeve and Graeme Hick would be classified as being as fit as Graham, yet they are all ten or more years younger. Mickey Stewart told me initially that some of the players would be negative towards the kind of schedules we set them but these have been easier for us to implement because the captain is so keen on fitness. I'm sure Graham will keep himself in trim for the rest of his life.'

The contrast with his contemporaries remained marked (and remarked upon): John Emburey, to take just one instance, would take out his car to journey from the pavilion to the indoor nets at Lord's. Gooch would complement the training schedule laid down by the Human

Performance Centre for all the England squad, under-taking exercises in his own gym. A typical week's sched-ule as dictated from Lilleshall would be: first session: varied pace run: 4 mins jog, 3 mins steady, 2 mins jog, 3 mins to include one 50 metre fast burst every 30 secs, 2 mins jog, 3 mins steady to include one 20 metre sprint every 30 secs, 2 mins jog, 2 mins fast, 4 mins jog to finish. Second session: gym/home circuit: 20 secs on 10 exercises ranging from squat thrusts to tennis ball squeezes, 20 secs rest, 3 circuits of exercises. Third ses-sion: 3 miles steady run. Fourth session: 4 mins steady run, 6 mins hard, 4 mins steady, 6 mins hard, 5 mins slow jog. For Gooch, this would be just the start.

To counter the weariness he would sometimes feel on the field, Gooch would take Sanatogen multi-vitamins; and in New Zealand he did not always make a track-suited start to the day. He realised it would be sensible to pace himself, not least in one-day cricket. And once England had made certain of winning the three-match limited-overs internationals, he dropped himself down the order, which Dexter suggested he should do as another means of extending his career.

The only thing that was not propitious about the start of the tour was Gooch's own fielding. In England's first match against a side of 'emerging' young players, he missed two catches off Tufnell. Doubtless both appreci-ated the irony in the light of Tufnell's inept fielding dis-plays the previous winter. Nevertheless, the spinner still took five wickets, enabling England to win by an innings. He also managed to shrug off newspaper allegations of throwing that were not supported by New Zealand's Board. Gooch was adamant that there was nothing wrong with Tufnell's action and was also coming round to the opinion that there was less awry with his character.

The young rebel was fast maturing, on and off the pitch and the surliness which had previously soured his relationship with Gooch was being replaced by mutual respect. Tufnell might even have been grateful for a kick up the backside – which was what his omission during the summer effectively had been.

Gooch had allowed Alec Stewart, his nominated vice-captain, to lead the side in this match. As ever, he was looking ahead, intent that England should be planning for the day he retired: he had already emphasised his unwillingness to tour India in the winter of 1992–3. Evidently he had had much to do with the choice of Stewart, who had been appointed ahead of Pringle and, for that matter, Botham. Gooch resumed the captaincy for the drawn match against a New Zealand Minor Associations Eleven, playing a dismissive innings of 42. He followed this with 47 in the first one-day international at Nelson, putting on 64 with Hick at a run a ball. England won by the commanding margin of seven wickets. Against a New Zealand Eleven he made 3 and, batting at number six in the second innings, 64, his intention being to give Mark Ramprakash more practice than he had gained hitherto. England won this encounter by two wickets. Gooch was now saying, almost *ad nauseam*, that if they played to their potential, they could beat anyone.

The words were commonplace, but they rang true. England's superiority over New Zealand was apparent once the first Test in Christchurch was underway. Astonishingly, though, given the events of the previous two years, this superiority was possible without a meaningful contribution from Gooch himself. In his first Test in New Zealand, the captain was the only England batsman to be dismissed for a score in single figures – that in a total of 580 for nine declared. He had made just two when he touched a leg-cutter from Danny Morrison to Ian Smith. Thereafter he was able to watch contentedly as Stewart, Robin Smith, Lamb, Lewis and Reeve all made substantial scores. He was still more contented when Tufnell began to exert a mesmeric influence on batsmen who had too little experience of playing top-class spin bowling. New Zealand were dismissed for 312, Tufnell taking four wickets.

Now, time was of the essence. Fifteen minutes after tea on the final day, New Zealand, following on, had reached 211 for 3. Their two best batsmen were together, only two wickets had fallen all day and the match was as good as drawn. Even Gooch, who normally would have reckoned that anything was possible, agreed that taking seven wickets in less than two hours was 'unrealistic'. What happened was that the match turned on a splendid piece of bowling by Tufnell. John Wright, marooned and fretting on 99, was lured down the pitch and stumped as he aimed to procure the necessary single. Thereupon New Zealand lost their next six wickets for 39 runs before Martin Crowe, aided by Chris Pringle, looked to have the match saved. Ten minutes remained when Crowe, needing four runs to level the scores (there was no time for England to bat again) gambled – and lost everything. Not quite to the pitch of a flighted ball from Tufnell, he sliced it high to deepish mid-off where the other Pringle, Derek, took the catch with supreme nonchalance. Tufnell's figures were 7 for 47 in 46 overs. 'On a pitch as bland as this, few other bowlers in the world could have conjured a result from the game, and Tufnell did so only through what Gooch chose to call "staying power",' wrote Alan Lee.

To be an Englishman and arrive the day after such a victory was ill-planned indeed. That Ian Botham was the visitor in question only illuminated this. Freed from his pantomime in Bournemouth, he provided the tabloid press with the *enfant terrible* they desired following Tufnell's reformation. Evidently carrying some surplus weight, he was not seen to be making the right PR moves in terms of fitness. England's management were reckoned to be slightly miffed that on an official day off soon after he arrived, he opted to play golf. The stinging criticism this drew from the pen of Geoffrey Boycott, who suggested Botham's stomach was too big and his appetite for work too small, was highly embarrassing for Gooch. If the captain could be said to have a guru, it was Boycott: now, Gooch and other England batsmen were unsure of whether they would be able to approach Boycott for help in the nets again. In the event, the manager put on a diplomatic front, stating publicly that Botham had volunteered to have a net. Gooch, worldly-wise in these matters, stayed clear of comment. Soon he was back in the nets under Boycott's guidance – and with Botham standing by, quietly seething.

There was some humour, too. Botham's first match was against Central Districts. Gooch chose again to play only as a batsman – he made just 8, his second successive score in single figures – and was given more overs to bowl by Alec Stewart than he would ideally have chosen. Upon taking the ball Gooch found Botham had moved the bowling marker so that he lost his run-up: his response was to balloon his next ball in the direction of the sniggering Botham at first slip, Gooch had showed he could take a joke on the field. He was also mischievously invited by Stewart to commute between fine leg and third man. Of more cerebral interest was the news from home that a group of academics from Essex University wanted Gooch to receive an honorary degree. Alas, it was soon possible to divine that England's cricket captain had been turned down. A spokesman for the University would not divulge the real reason. 'It would be the same if you rang Downing Street and asked why Fred Bloggs hadn't got the OBE,' was the cryptic response. As somebody asked: 'Bloggs? Who did he play for?'

Mortar and Board, though, were of less concern to Gooch than scoring runs. His form in New Zealand had been patchy. 'It is a slight concern but no more,' he said on the eve of the second Test in Auckland. 'I think my mental approach to batting is as good now as it has ever been. I go in expecting to do well.' He said so even though he had had time to take stock of the pitch, one of a sickly lime green. Suspecting the worst, he had for several days told his players that the psychology of playing on a poor pitch was never to consider the odds. The surface was damp as well, so it was no surprise that upon winning the toss New Zealand put England in. The start was delayed, whereupon three wickets were lost in eight balls. Gooch, pushing out at a leg-cutter from Morrison, edged to the wicket-keeper. Stewart, who had so amply fulfilled his captain's hopes in the first Test, now went for 4 and Smith was also out to Chris Cairns, playing across a late outswinger. That England finished with 203 had much to do with dropped catches.

This had been a calculated gamble by New Zealand to play on a sub-standard pitch, one taken by many a country before them when faced with stronger opposition. It now backfired. With Lewis taking five wickets, England dismissed New Zealand for 142. Other than Crowe, their batsmen simply did not look the part in such conditions. Gooch had always been quick to deride the idea that the series could be belittled as merely a warm-up for the World Cup and now he was to prove his point in telling fashion. He put his opponents out of the game – and out of the series – with a century that was memorable for its resolve. It emphasised that only a really great batsman makes such a score when out of form.

For the first time on the tour he played like a man short of confidence rather than merely short of runs. Numerous times Morrison beat him outside off stump, his feet were slow to move into position and his bat was so far from coming down straight that Boycott described him on the air as 'nervy and anxious'. His first 50 runs took three hours. He faced 133 balls, exactly 100 more than Lamb needed for a punchy half-century, an innings that was invaluable for its rapid counter-attack. This, and the fact that Gooch made his second 50 in little more than an hour, was all the more remarkable in view of the extreme variance in bounce. Gooch had made 114 in 294 minutes with fifteen fours and two sixes when he was absurdly run out by Reeve. Gooch had no hope of reaching the striker's end, not even attempting to run his bat in. Other captains might well have given vent to their feelings: Gooch merely trudged off, aware, no doubt, that the match was as good as won. England finished with a total of 321, which left New Zealand the notional task of making 383 to win; and in spite of a half-century by Crowe, the series was soon decided.

England's triumph, by 168 runs, gave them their first victory in a series overseas since 1987 and their first in New Zealand since 1975 under Mike Denness, who was at Auckland. There was praise – and frank talking – for Gooch from Boycott. 'I can take umbrage with Graham over only one thing, because I'm very fond of him. He said you needed a lot of luck on that pitch. What you needed was a lot of ability.' Typically, Gooch chose his moment – one of jubilation – to pass a comment of some depression. Six months short of his thirty-ninth birthday, he hinted again that this would be his last overseas tour. 'There is not much petrol left in the tank,' he said. 'I still love playing but at my pensionable age it takes longer to recover from each match. Once you start to lose it a bit, there is no coming back.' Evidently Gooch was discovering that the rigorous physical standards he set himself were almost beyond a man close to forty. Minor injuries were now harder to shake off, and he was finding that it was best to cut down on road-running to protect an injured knee and that an old hand injury might be connected with his missing a number of sharp chances. He was musing over all this as the chairman of the England committee arrived in New Zealand.

Dexter immediately made it clear that Gooch could have the following winter off if he so wished, insisting there had been precedents for allowing a captain to take time off – not least when he himself stood down from touring India in 1963–4. Mike Smith led the side, Dexter returning to lead England the following summer. 'I can understand the older family man getting unhappy at being away from home again,' said Dexter. 'But Graham always tends to look on the gloomy side of things. When he wags his head and tells us he's not going on much longer, I think he's really talking to Brenda.' As for Gooch's success, Dexter said: 'Appointing Graham as captain was one of the best decisions I've ever made. He's become an expert at winning cricket matches. To win four Tests in succession is a magnificent achievement. Some people might think he can appear almost diffident at times. But don't be fooled. He is very determined, very single-minded and demands high standards from his team.' Dexter felt that Gooch's form with the bat would keep him going a while longer: his century at Auckland was his eighth in sixteen Tests: his previous eight had taken 77 matches. He put this down to having overcome only in the previous two years the psychological aspects of the game. 'I had missed out a few times and when you don't score runs your confidence can take a dent. But you keep believing in your ability. If you don't, you might as well not play, because you will never succeed.' Crowe, gracious in defeat, praised Gooch: 'I really admire Graham's desire to succeed. He wants to lead from the front all the time. We have seen him practising here at breakfast time every day of this game and, although we knew he had been in bad nick, we also knew he would fight it through.'

Gooch, and England, were now starting to turn their attention towards the imminent World Cup. For all the captain's protestations that the series against New Zealand was never going to be looked upon merely as a string of warm-up matches, Dexter emphasised that the squad had been selected with the one-day tournament in mind. First, though, there was one more Test as well as two further one-day internationals to be played against New Zealand.

Wellington was the venue for the Test and, of not least significance, Botham's 100th cap. For the first time in the series Gooch won the toss. Opting to bat without total conviction on another unworthy, mottled pitch, he was promptly dropped twice in the first six overs. It was not, though, the extravagant movement that accounted for his dismissal but the off-spin of Dipak Patel, who captured England's first four wickets. Gooch's stroke was uncharacteristic in that again he suffered from uncertain footwork in advancing to drive. He was well from the pitch of the ball, which turned sharply and bowled him through the gate. He had made 30. Fortunately for him, Stewart, with whom he had put on 83, scored his second century of the series, England mustering 305. Centuries by John Wright and Andrew Jones enabled New Zealand to declare with a lead of 127, achieved as Gooch, not surprisingly, looked increasingly hangdog in the field. When he batted a second time he was soon out to a lifting ball from Cairns, again uncharacteristically failing to get over it and steering a catch to gully. His two dismissals in this match were the shots of an enervated man.

As in the first innings, a century-maker enabled England to keep New Zealand at bay and, indeed, to draw the match. Lamb's 142 was his highest score in the 77 Tests he had played, and mightily combative it was, too. The match, though, had by now been overshadowed by a fearful injury to David Lawrence, England's pugilistic fast bowler, who broke his left kneecap in his delivery stride during the final session. The match may have been meandering to a draw, but he knew of only one way to bowl: wholeheartedly. As he was borne off on a stretcher by half the England team, a Television New Zealand cameraman, Vaughan Scott, attempting to film the visual and audible agony, was pushed aside by Mickey Stewart and pursued up a flight of steps by Jack Russell. Botham inevitably had his say. Gooch, equally inevitably, maintained a discreet profile.

Lawrence was given immediate surgery in the hope of saving his career before being flown home to join the BSkyB World Cup commentary team. In the two remaining one-day internationals, both of which were won by England, Gooch scored 24 and, again choosing to bat down the order as well as give the captaincy to Alec Stewart, an unbeaten 22. It was a pleasing way to end his cricket in a country to which he would not be returning as a player. His remarks about his tank empty-ing of petrol could be interpreted as appeasing Brenda, or of failing confidence, or of impending retirement, or indeed of all three. He had been ambiguous, pessimistic and depressive about his intentions in the past. Realism returned when he gave an interview to the *Mail on Sunday* at the end of the tour. 'I'd like to believe I can go on for some time to come. I still believe I can perform better than most and at the moment I'm coping all right. A lot of people may disagree with my methods. I'm not saying I have all the right answers. But if the people who put me in this position don't like it, they can always get someone to replace me. I wouldn't hang on if I felt I couldn't do the job – that would be difficult to handle. But I want to go on as long as possible because you're a long time retired.'

13

Third Time Unlucky

If the fifth World Cup was essentially a victory for Pakistan's volatile individualism over the solid professionalism of the Gooch–Stewart regime, it was also a captivating tournament in its sheer unpredictability. For Gooch, there was defeat and, in spite of reaching the final, dejection: he cut the most sorrowful of figures as Imran Khan gave a victory speech that dwelt more on his cancer hospital campaign than Pakistan's cricket. To be on the losing side in a final on one occasion is hard to take; to be so three times is a record of sorts that is unlikely to be broken.

With the bat, Gooch had mixed success, starting with a spate of half-centuries and finishing with a string of low scores. In the field he felt his age, as he had done in New Zealand. Still he could not free himself of injury, missing two of the matches in the preliminary rounds owing to a pulled hamstring, although that did not impair England's efficient progress to the final. Of his significant innings, his half-century against India was a crucial contribution to a nine-run victory and was followed five days later by 65 against West Indies, the highest score of England's innings and, indeed, the match. The margin of victory, six wickets, was an achievement in itself.

Of England's first five matches, four were won and

none lost. After bowling out Pakistan – without Imran – for 74, they were defeated only by the weather. Here, Gooch made three, his wicket the only one to fall before England's innings was curtailed by rain. Then, in a memorable eight-wicket win over Australia in which Botham made an inspired all-round contribution, a further half-century. Such form was disrupted only by injury. Gooch missed England's initial victory over South Africa and defeat by New Zealand, returning to be out to the very first ball of the innings against Zimbabwe. Defeat, albeit by only nine runs, told much about the levelling of ability among the Test-playing countries.

England, though, had achieved quite enough to reach the semi-finals. Indeed, they and New Zealand were considered favourites, for Pakistan were still too mercurial for their own good. In Sydney England played South Africa in a match which throughout was sufficiently compelling to be one of the more memorable limited-overs contests – though as it turned out it was remembered for the wrong reasons. Television, something of a monster in Australia since Kerry Packer's time, was to blame. Regulations were drawn up that in the event of rain would favour not the cricket but the scheduling of the programmes to be shown afterwards. The side batting second would have to chase a revised target against the clock to ensure that soap operas duly appeared on time.

Needless to say, this match became not so much soap opera as comic strip. In sending England in on a day when clouds were banked was a calculated gamble by South Africa that did not come off. The weather and their over rate were such that England batted for just 45 overs, reaching 252 for six. Gooch was again beaten by the new ball, Allan Donald having him caught at the wicket for two. Although the total was a substantial one, only Hick, with 83 from 90 balls, made a big score. South Africa's reply, resilient though it was, never quite matched the asking rate, even if 22 from 13 balls with four wickets intact was clearly feasible. But then, of course, came the rain. After a brief stoppage and numerous consultations, South Africa's target was revised. It was decreed that they needed 21 off one ball, an asking rate that even Jessop would have found tricky. To their immense credit, South Africa accepted their fate in this ludicrous fiasco with remarkably good grace. It was just as well that Australia had not been batting at the time.

Thankfully, not least for the organisers, the final in Melbourne was played in balmy conditions with scant sign of cloud. For England, debilitated by injury and wearied by one flight after another, it came a fortnight or so too late. Their best form was behind them, whereas Pakistan, even without Waqar Younis, were on a crescendo. Imran had likened them to cornered tigers, telling his players they had nowhere to go other than to scrap for runs and wickets.

Imran respected Gooch as much for his honesty as for his ability but could not understand his lack of self-belief – a characteristic Imran himself never lacked. In the final it was all too apparent in Pakistan's cricket, even when the captain and Javed Miandad were managing just four runs from the bat in 60 balls. Their strategy, after the openers were out cheaply, was to consolidate to the extent of not concerning themselves unduly with the scoring rate. Wickets in hand would be all-important. After 34 overs Pakistan had mustered only 113 runs, albeit for the loss of only two wickets; but in the next 16 they hammered 136. Imran finished on 72, having been dropped on nine – by Gooch – and Pakistan with 249 for six from their 50 overs. That chance to Gooch was a hard one, the ball swirling out of a multi-coloured backdrop of 87,000 spectators. Would he have caught it five, ten years before? Probably not.

The difference in the approach of the two sides was highlighted by the use of their slow bowlers. Imran used Mushtaq as an attacking leg spinner, whereas Richard Illingworth was played for flat trajectory, containment and lack of risk. The difference was encapsulated in the googly with which Mushtaq had Hick leg before, for no batsman could have appeared so thoroughly bamboozled. This was but one of three cheap wickets England lost in struggling towards a target that had looked as if it was a good 20 runs beyond them. 'Imran's playing of Mushtaq was a really bold decision and the difference between the two sides on the day,' said Gooch. 'We hardly ever play bowlers of his type in England, so it's difficult.' He might have added the name of Wasim Akram, who clubbed 33 at a vital stage in Pakistan's innings and took important wickets whenever needed to do so. The margin of Pakistan's victory, 22 runs, flattered England.

In that Gooch's expression in defeat will invariably be woebegone to the point of hangdog, he is as inconsolable as most sportsmen of the modern age. Yet he is not a bad loser. He accepted the result with good grace, even if his drooping shoulders on the podium told all. At the interminable press conferences, post-match and at Heathrow, he was platitudinous and pleasant, though inevitably unresponsive to any banal, uninformed question. Then he was off around the M25 to his beloved Essex.

There was only just time for a family holiday before the rigours of another season. Gooch had become honorary captain and part-time coach at Barringtons, a sporting club in the Algarve close to his villa. When he put on his pads, he found the captain of Spain and Portugal's military medium-pacers not quite so taxing as Imran Khan and Wasim Akram. What was demanding was the unrelenting schedule of the modern cricketer. The World Cup final was played on 25 March, a time when Essex were about to report back for pre-season training, and by mid-April the new season was under way. Some England players in Gooch's position would not have bothered to turn out for Essex against England A at Lord's in temperatures that bore no resemblance to Melbourne or Vale do Lobo: he, as ever, put his country first. He began the match averaging 49.90 in all his cricket at Lord's and finished it a degree or two higher, having made 74 off 122 balls.

Form and fortune followed in equal measure. In May, an innings of 160 for Essex against Leicestershire. Then only nine and 25 in the first two one-day internationals against Pakistan, but both finished in victory for England. In directing from the deep field, he may often have seemed like a semaphore, but if nothing more, this was better than losing to the same country in the World Cup final.

Pakistan were already ruing the absence of Imran. Indeed, England's total of 302 for five in this second match was their highest in any one-day international against Pakistan. Even now, though, no one could be certain of the true capabilities of their opponents. If, with every passing day, Imran was less likely to appear on the tour, then Waqar and Wasim were increasingly looking as if they could escape their injuries. One, but not both, was fit for the first Test at Edgbaston, on the eve of which Gooch made a plea for an improvement in behaviour. He said that players had to face punishment for misconduct after one warning rather than the two tacitly allowed under the International Cricket Council's Code of

Conduct. 'I now make a habit of telling umpires that anyone stepping out of line should get only one warning and then he is in trouble. There is latitude for two warnings in the Code but I don't think that's right,' said Gooch. The Test itself finished in a high-scoring draw, Gooch confessing afterwards that he had chosen wrongly in not selecting a leg-spinner in Ian Salisbury. Salim Malik and Javed Miandad made large centuries as, for England, did Alec Stewart and Smith. Gooch mustered eight in his one innings.

The second Test was a more even contest between bat and ball, the course of it thoroughly enervating. In making 69 in a highly attractive first wicket partnership of 123 with Stewart, Gooch batted as if his regulation century at Lord's was a formality. Timing and strength were conspicuous allies. Then, as if distracted by an announcement that Essex had been beaten by an innings at Headingley, he went back to a quicker ball from Wasim and was bowled off the inside edge. After this splendid start, England's total of 255 was considerably less than anticipated. For if ever a Test was decided by a pair of fast bowlers, it was now. Waqar took five wickets in England's first innings and Wasim four in their second. On a pitch of greater turn and bounce than was customary, Pakistan were left needing 138 to win and nine hours in which to make them. Gooch, weaned on the Essex psyche of never anticipating failure, tried finger-wagging pep talks and each of such fit bowlers as he had, which effectively meant only three. Lewis and Salisbury gained three wickets apiece but the match was fittingly decided by Wasim and Waqar. Their unbeaten ninth wicket stand of 46 enabled Pakistan to win by eight wickets with a day to spare.

Memorable Test though it was, suspicions of ball-tampering were already rife. Later in the summer this would become the most controversial topic of a series that was hardly short of them. Other than that, there was the little matter of Gooch's relationship with Gower, which resurfaced when the former's treatise on captaincy was published early in the season. 'Under my captaincy for England, I believe David hasn't shown a good attitude or given enough to the rest of the team,' wrote Gooch. 'The younger ones quite rightly look up to him and respect what he has achieved but he needed to set a better example to them and he didn't, especially in Australia.'

To stave off criticism that his prime concern was five-mile runs and sweating buckets in the nets, Gooch emphasised that he had been bothered more by the danger of England players developing splinter groups. At the end of that summer Gower would produce an account of his own, an autobiography that was at odds with the regimentation of Gooch and, in particular, Mickey Stewart. Somehow, though, they remained reasonably good friends. And in England, at any rate, Gooch wanted Gower in his side – providing, of course, he made some runs in county cricket. The third Test at Old Trafford was the venue for Gower's return – and a significant return it was, too. During a match spoiled by rain, Gower displaced Geoffrey Boycott as England's most prolific run-maker, scoring 73 out of a total of 390. In grim light Gooch had to make three starts to his own innings. He was dropped twice in the slips but gathered 78 before fencing at Waqar to give a catch behind.

It was piquant that he was partnering Gower when the milestone was passed. 'Graham said well done. Quite succinct – but his main concern was that I'd be looking at a bigger total,' said Gower. In the event, it hardly mattered. The match fizzled out with Pakistan barely having time to build on their 115-run lead or make amends for their petulance about umpiring strictures over short-pitched bowling and the scuffed condition of the ball. In their second innings Gooch was England's most effective bowler, taking two for 30 in the month of his thirty-ninth birthday. He would have much preferred it had a younger man taken the wickets.

The Pakistanis' behaviour at Old Trafford, especially when Aqib Javed reacted childishly after bowling three bouncers in succession at Devon Malcolm, had led to further strictures, these from Conrad Hunte, the ICC match referee. Umpire Palmer had needed a police escort off the field and Hunte's report had unintentionally linked Gooch by implication with these shabby events. On the eve of the fourth Test at Headingley Gooch hand-delivered a letter of protest to Sir Colin Cowdrey, ICC's chairman. Not only was he irked at the association with unseemly behaviour, he was annoyed at the way Aqib ran through the crease to intimidate Malcolm. Hunte apologised, saying England's attitude was 'exemplary'.

As if buoyed by this, Gooch was 93 not out by the end of the second day, on the ground where the previous year he had carried his bat for 154 against West Indies. Again the pitch was of low, treacherous bounce. While Essex were dismissed for 75 at Grace Road, Gooch went on to complete 135 out of England's total of 320, with a six and 19 fours. His ninth century in 21 Tests since being made captain proved to be as significant an innings as that at Headingley the previous year, for it led to England's first victory over Pakistan for ten years – and with a day to spare. Gooch's previous 77 Test matches produced only eight centuries: now, he moved ahead of Clive Lloyd into the ranks of the ten highest run-scorers in Test cricket. Pakistan were bowled out for 197 and 221, Neil

Mallender making the kind of debut that on a different pitch would have been the harbinger of a longer Test career. Left needing 99 to win in conditions that were deteriorating by the over, England gained them for the loss of six wickets. Those were the bald statistics – the reality was that it was much closer. This was a dour struggle against a high-class attack. Gooch's score of 37 was worth much more.

Other centuries followed: an unbeaten 105 off Gloucestershire in a NatWest quarter-final at Cheltenham that Essex won, and 141 against the Pakistanis at Chelmsford, an innings and, indeed, a match that one or two other England batsmen would have deemed of scant importance even at a time when the first-class counties were near-ordered to field full sides.

So to the Oval and the deciding match of a pulsating Test series. For Gooch there were two low scores – 20 and 24 – but the salient factor in England's defeat was the extraordinary ability of Wasim and Waqar to use an old ball as if it were brand new. 'I have never known anyone swing the ball so much at that pace,' admitted Gooch. Throughout the summer, the England captain never once made any allegation of ball-tampering, unlike Allan Lamb or even Mickey Stewart, who refused to comment at the end of this Test as to whether the Pakistanis' method of making the old ball swing came within the laws of the game. Whatever, England could not cope. Bowled out for 207 and 174, they were beaten by a team in which almost every batsman made a worthwhile contribution.

There was some heartening news for England, or so it appeared at the time. Gooch delighted Keith Fletcher, Stewart's successor, by telling him he would lead the tour to India and Sri Lanka that winter. He professed this was principally to give succour to his old friend and mentor. Dexter's view had long been that Gooch would come round to the tour, that any statement expressing doubt was merely his method of opening negotiations with Brenda. It was reckoned at the time that Fletcher had persuaded Gooch to tour and, later in the year, that Brenda was trying to make him change his mind. But the truth of the matter was that Gooch, as always, was his own man.

There remained of his season three one-day internationals and a NatWest semi-final and a Championship to be decided. A conclusive victory over Pakistan at Trent Bridge, in which Gooch scored 42, enabled him to drop out of the next match at Lord's in order to get over a troublesome hand injury. At Old Trafford he made 45 in another victory so straightforward that it was beginning to seem as if Pakistan's World Cup victory was either a considerable fluke or owed more to Imran Khan than they would care to admit.

For Gooch, as for the majority of cricketers, the Championship was still the trophy to win. Essex, even in Gooch's absences, were the strongest county with the greatest strength in depth: they lost their NatWest semi-final to Leicestershire but had never not looked like becoming champions. Their sixth Championship since 1979 was achieved, appropriately enough, in their final match at Chelmsford, where they beat Hampshire. 'We play to entertain,' Gooch told the delirious crowd. 'You know that. You keep watching and we'll try to keep winning.' He was as good as his word. In their penultimate match at Derby, Essex made 440 to win, of which Gooch made an unbeaten century coming in at number six. It was, as he laconically described it, 'a top-drawer performance' and the most satisfying victory in county cricket of his career. In their final match at Bristol, he again handed the captaincy to Paul Prichard and went in down the order, this time not for reasons to do with where he would bat come middle age but because of a mountain of correspondence that awaited his attention. The upshot was the same: another century, even if on this occasion Gooch could not carry Essex to victory.

Autumn came and went with no respite in his heavy schedule. Opportunities for after-dinner speaking were as lucrative as before. A trip to Portugal was not merely for a family holiday and enquiries into buying a bigger villa but for further coaching sessions. Stewart joined him to contemplate the possibility of England practising there before their forthcoming winter tours.

On returning to England, Gooch attended the unveiling of a statue of himself in Chelmsford, not demurring at the unorthodox shot he was depicted to be playing. Brenda faithfully accompanied him. It was all the more extraordinary, then, that within a few weeks their marriage was declared to be not merely in difficulties but over. As Peter Edwards said, you could imagine this happening to numerous other couples, but never to Graham and Brenda. The tabloid headlines 'You're out!' did not seem credible. In one sense they were not: Brenda had not given her husband an ultimatum over the tour of India, as was originally supposed (or imagined) by the newspaper whose reporter had overheard Gooch telling Fletcher of his decision to leave home. John Emburey, his closest friend, knew nothing of it – and neither did anyone else.

The story broke on the eve of England's departure to India, an ominous start to the tour. In Shenfield, Brenda's house was under siege. Everyone wanted to know what truth there was in the revelation. And the *News of the World* was prepared to use the cheque book. It transpired that a fortnight before Christmas Graham told her and the children that he would not be returning home after coming back from India. 'Two years ago Graham and I were sitting together in front of the TV when he suddenly said he was unhappy with me. It was very civilised. I felt like bursting into tears or screaming but I did my best to keep calm,' said Brenda.

'We struggled on for a year and again I tried to iron out our problems but it was no good. Graham had made up his mind. Of course I wondered if he had someone else. It must cross every wife's mind. But I realised with a sinking heart it really was because he didn't love me any more.' She said she had never given him an ultimatum in her life. The reality was that they had grown apart. The shy individual from Leytonstone had no more need of mollycoddling. He drank fine wines, lunched at Buckingham Palace; his milieu was now the stockbroker belt. Brenda's preferred life was Tesco and school runs.

Apart from the effect on the children, perhaps the saddest aspect of all was that as the tour of India was to be Gooch's last, he would have every chance to see more of his family. Yet there seemed to be scant chance of a reconciliation. Once Gooch's mind was made up, he could be notoriously stubborn. Brenda's hope was that he would miss the children sufficiently not to want to leave them once he was back in England.

It was, of course, hardly the ideal start to a tour on which everything that could possibly go wrong did. With the benefit of hindsight, England underestimated India, both in terms of their own on-field performance in their own country and the sheer debility brought on by living there for ten weeks. Gooch was rarely fit. On the few occasions when he was, he was generally out of form. Even when he scored a century in the run-up to the first Test it was shrouded in controversy. This should have been the 100th of his career, but with the ICC coming to the strange conclusion that a century he made in South Africa in 1982 was not first-class (although the bowling certainly was) he was left, tantalisingly, with 99. His 100th Test, the first of the series, would have been the fitting occasion on which to score his 100th hundred. But by then the tour was going horribly wrong.

When England lost the first of the one-day inter-nationals, in Chandigarh, it was a defeat that had more bearing on the Test series than would most such matches. On India's tour of South Africa Mohammed Azharuddin had been criticised as an indifferent captain unable to motivate his side under trying circumstances. Not only did he bolster his confidence with the one-day victory, but he played a magnificent innings of 182 in the first Test at Calcutta. His spinners, Kumble – disparagingly judged by Fletcher – Raju and Chaihan, then won him the match. Gooch's contribution was 17 in England's dis-mal first innings total of 163 and 18 before he was need-lessly stumped off Kumble when they followed on. Only Gatting, who reached 81, delayed defeat for long.

Worse was to come. Gooch had already suffered from a virus during the tour, and was barely fit for the first Test, but his next ailment was still more debilitating. He opted to eat in the Chinese restaurant of England's (smart) hotel in Madras on the eve of the second Test. Given that the city is on the coast, shellfish would have seemed an appealing alternative to endless curry. What occurred, though, between the catching and the preparation of prawns was another matter. Gooch was not the only Eng-land cricketer to throw up his Chinese meal that night –

but he was the only one to miss the Test. Of still greater discomfort to him was his side's performance without him. As they say in the part of Essex he comes from: they were stuffed.

Strong words emanated from captain and manager alike before the final Test in Bombay. The series was lost, yet 'pride' was a word liberally bandied about. In that Graeme Hick made his first Test century, such words had their effect. The result, though, was no different: defeat by an innings. For Gooch, scores of four and eight had everything to do with his physical and mental state and nothing to do with his tank running out of petrol. The sheer numbing mediocrity of the England perform-ance was doubtless beginning to haunt him. If blame attached itself to him, as it would do, this stemmed more from his decision to tour in the first place and the omis-sion of Gower than what he achieved with the bat. The party was chosen with one-day cricket in mind and yet the results – three wins apiece – would soon be forgotten. It would be quite different with the Tests.

14

England Scuppered

For Gooch to admit he had made a mistake in going to India was one thing. To admit it publicly was another. He had been stoical about his illness and had had no wish to use it as an excuse for poor cricket, though to everyone else it had been a glaringly obvious reason for England's poor performances. In the spring of 1993 he was not at all certain that he wanted to remain as captain – assuming, of course, that he was reappointed. He had returned to England, earlier than the rest of the party, to a failed marriage and a new life at the cottage he was having renovated close to his old home. The tank, he repeatedly asserted, was running out of petrol.

Yet Gooch was soon sufficiently rejuvenated to talk openly of wanting to lead England throughout the forthcoming series against Australia. This was in spite of declaring that he had no wish to tour West Indies again the following winter. 'I would have thought beating Australia was the most important thing on the agenda,' he said. 'I don't think we should be worrying about West Indies just yet.' Dexter, loyal to a fault, agreed, reappointing Gooch as captain – but not for the entire series. Gooch, for his part, realised he could expect nothing more. 'After what happened in the winter, the selectors were entitled to appoint me for only half the series,' he admitted.

At least he had the kind of job security for which other national leaders, the Prime Minister and Norman Lamont among them, would have given much in the face of constant defeat. Yet as Alan Lee wrote in *The Times*, 'to Gooch there was no satisfaction to be had from being the indispensable captain of a badly holed ship'. By the end of the Texaco one-day matches it appeared scuppered.

Australia won the first match at Old Trafford by four runs, the second at Edgbaston by as much as six wickets in spite of Robin Smith hitting one of the finest centuries in the history of one-day cricket, and, far from sated, were victorious in the third at Lord's by 19 runs. Gooch's contributions in the face of such hostile bowling as Craig McDermott managed before injury ended his tour, were 4, 17 and 42. He was as alarmed by his own lack of form as of that of his side. In seventeen innings in Tests and one-day internationals he had not made a half-century. So, rather than repine at home or seek solace in the nets, Gooch opted to play for Essex Second Eleven for the first time in twenty years. He had never been dropped by Essex; now he was, so to speak, demoting himself. The venue was Castle Park, Colchester, devoid of its customary tents, atmosphere, reality. There were more journalists than spectators. In sixty-five minutes' batting against Somerset he made 25 before he was lbw to one Andrew Payne. Taciturn as ever, he had just six words for the massed scribes: 'I enjoyed my day's cricket, OK?'

Whether or not he was enjoying the new four-day championship format was another matter, for he was having all too few innings. The extra practice was necessary. And come the first Test at Old Trafford Gooch had dispelled any suspicion that he was playing for England only because he was captain. He made 65 in the first innings and 133 in the second, one of his finest Test centuries. Yet such achievement was completely overshadowed. It was not simply that England were beaten by 179 runs – Merv Hughes and Shane Warne taking the wickets, just about everybody making runs – or that Gooch became the first Englishman in Test cricket to be out for handling the ball, knocking it away with his right hand as it bounced towards his leg stump. It was the manner of defeat which riled.

'If things don't improve, it would not be right for me to carry on,' said Gooch. 'If I can't have the desired effect on players, someone else should try.' England's poor cricket had conflicted with everything he stood for, everything, indeed, on which his leadership depended. 'It is not that people don't try,' he said. 'Nobody sets out to lose. But we have reached a stage where it is being accepted far too easily. We have had a bad trot and if a game begins to drift, as it did at Old Trafford, I can sense players thinking they have seen it all before and just going through the motions. I have wondered whether it is me, whether I am to blame for being unable to motivate them properly. But, really, no one should need motivating to play for England. It should mean as much to them as it does to me. It should mean everything. I am not interested in the kudos of captaining England – it has no appeal for me. My motivation is winning, doing my best as a player and getting other people to compete. If I can't do that, there is no point in me doing the job. I have a way of doing things which has worked for Essex and didn't exactly fail for England. But I can't bat and bowl for the others. They have to do their bit and they have to want to win as much as I do.'

Gooch had been aware, too, that the same complacent

attitude was affecting Essex. Perhaps it was inevitable given that they had won the Championship two years in succession. Gooch called his players together and told them they were looking more like also-rans than champions. They had responded well, he felt. 'The thing that has been worrying me more than anything about English cricket is the lack of mental fibre,' he said. 'It doesn't matter enough when things go badly. There is an attitude that there will always be another day.

'That is what is wrong with our game, where we are failing to compete with teams like Australia. For them, every game is special. It would have been valuable to have drawn the first Test for the psychological lift it would have given us. And really, we should have saved it. We have the talent. All we needed was for somebody to hang around and make 50 or 60.'

Gooch was aware of how well he had played during that innings of 133, made with twenty-one fours and two sixes. He had played well enough, it transpired, to be given the captaincy for the remainder of the series. This was partly, no doubt, because there was no other contender for the role but also because he was viewed as the one person who could inspire others, even if that was largely through his batting. It also lifted the pressure on him to drop down the order. He himself gave the credit for his positive outlook at the crease to Sir Gary Sobers, whom he had met by chance at a benefit dinner. 'I told him I was struggling a bit and he said I should not worry but just remind myself that I was a top player and go out and play my shots. He was right, too, because if you are not positive you cannot be in the frame of mind to put away the half-volley.'

Gooch had been considerably helped by having, as a kind of personal travelling coach, Alan Lilley, who would help him not so much over his technique as to whether he was moving into the correct positions. Footwork had, of course, been Gooch's particular difficulty against the Australians in 1989. Golfers and tennis players had their own coaches so there was no reason, Gooch felt, why he should not benefit as well. He had started a daily 'flexibility programme' and was starting to bat for Essex in the middle order. As with Second Eleven cricket, this too he had not done since the 1970s.

'It will be easier for me to bat down the order and will give the county a chance to try someone new,' he said. 'But timing is everything and I was intent on opening this year because, if I had not, it would have given out the wrong messages to people who would have assumed I was on my last legs.'

Nonetheless, his threat to resign if England's players did not show an improvement in their approach remained. In a sense, Gooch had boxed himself into a corner. When Australia won the second Test at Lord's by an innings and 62 runs, their superiority evident almost from the moment Michael Slater took guard on the first morning, the inevitable question was asked. And for once, Gooch did not make runs in a Test match at Lord's, mustering just 12 and 29. No, he said, he would not be resigning just yet. Besides, he had been reappointed just before the second Test so as to avoid speculation over the captaincy. The trouble was that the Australians kept on winning. And, in spite of not wanting to be seen as the old man moving down the order, Gooch chose to do just that for the third Test at Trent Bridge. Someone had to make way if Mark Lathwell was to be given his debut and Gooch decided it might just as well be him.

If this was also to give England greater strength in the

middle order, it worked. Although Gooch made no more than 38 when they batted first, Hughes troubling him by repeatedly digging the ball in short of a length at variable speed, he almost turned the match in the second innings. With Australia leading by 52 runs, he came to the wicket when – as ever – runs were direly needed. His riposte was to make his eleventh century in 27 Tests since resuming the captaincy, becoming the third Englishman after Boycott and Gower to reach 8,000 Test runs.

This was his nineteenth Test century in all and arguably his most important, since defeat would have resulted in Australia clinching the Ashes. His 120, which included a six and eighteen fours, ended only when Warne turned a leg-break wickedly out of the rough and had him taken at slip. England could not manage to take more than six Australian wickets before the match was drawn, but Gooch had made his point. 'It is good to know we were more competitive,' he said.

Alas, this lasted only until his fortieth birthday. The start of the fourth Test at Headingley rendered any further mention of the Ashes completely pointless. A double hundred by Border and centuries apiece by Steve Waugh and Boon enabled Australia to declare at 653 for four. In response, Gooch made 59 of England's measly total of 200 and then, when the outcome was more or less decided, played a frisky innings of 26 which ended when he was stumped charging down the pitch to the off-spin of Tim May. He was as jaunty off the field. This was the mood of a man whose mind was made up.

After England had been beaten by an innings and 148 runs, Gooch informed his side of the news they must have been suspecting for several days. He emerged from the dressing-room, unsmiling but far from emotional, to say that the Ashes had been conceded and thus the side would benefit from fresh ideas and a fresh approach. They needed, he said, 'someone else to look up to'. Since beating Pakistan at Headingley the previous year, England had lost eight matches out of nine, four of the defeats by an innings. They had not beaten Australia in seventeen attempts. 'I have considered it a great honour to captain England,' said Gooch. 'I can always look in the mirror and know I have always done my best for the team, but now it is right and proper that someone else should have a go.'

There was sympathy even from Border. 'If you lose, you cop it,' said the Australian captain. 'I've been there. But it saddens me for we are great mates. He's one of the greatest cricketers England have produced but I can fully understand his reasons for going. If your team are no longer giving a hundred per cent and are not responding, there is no option. Gooch can't do everything. He prepares for the job as well as anyone I've ever seen in the game but he's forty. He cannot bear to see others less committed than he is.'

His was not to be the only resignation. When England lost the fifth Test at Edgbaston under his successor, Mike Atherton, Ted Dexter decided that he, too, had had enough. Gooch had escaped being 'lampooned and harpooned', as Dexter put it, but both became victims of the constant desire to find scapegoats at a time of sporting stress. So an unlikely but worthy and quite often successful partnership had been split up. Given that England were by now 4–0 down in the series and the Ashes were irretrievable, it was bound to happen. The tabloid Press and, in the case of Dexter, his wife, only hastened the end.

Away from the prying lens, Gooch was a happier man. There was no question that Atherton would not want him in his side for the fifth Test, nor that he would do anything other than open the batting again. For his faltering Essex side, he made an unbeaten 159, his first championship century of the season, against Worcestershire in the preceding match. Without him they might well have lost a third successive match in the championship for the first time since 1987. In fact they gained their third victory of the season, which meant they should at least finish in a mid-table position.

As for the fifth Test, Gooch again showed that he was not merely the best batsman in England's side but, of greater relevance given the conditions, the best player of spin. He made only 8 in the first innings, following an out-swinger from Paul Reiffel to first slip, but 48, the second highest score, in a second-innings total of 251. He again played Warne better than anyone before he was bowled round his legs, unable to counter a ball that turned phenomenally. In Australia's second innings he fielded on the boundary for the first time in many years – although not for long since the visitors won by eight wickets, with plenty of time remaining in the day for Dexter to become the focus of attention.

A confusing summer for Gooch ended as confusingly for him as it did for England. In the sixth Test at the Oval, the 107th of his career, he became the most prolific English Test batsman, overtaking Gower's 8,231 runs. Characteristically, victory meant more to him than the record. In the first innings he made an exhilarating 56, batting as freely as he had at any time in Test cricket and enabling his side to make exactly the start they needed if they were to gain a consolation victory.

The much-awaited return of Angus Fraser, restored to opening the attack with Devon Malcolm, was equally dramatic. Between them they took eight wickets, giving

England a first-innings lead of 77. Thereupon Gooch, who had taken his 99th Test catch at short leg, of all extraordinary positions, hit the first ball of his second innings for four and broke Gower's record with another full-faced drive. Nothing was better than the extra-cover drive which followed, played off Tim May with one knee almost on the ground. His innings of 79 included thirteen fours and was ended only by a Warne leg-break which spun viciously out of the rough.

Gooch's reaction to all this heady excitement? Relief that his record-breaking achievement was at last out of the way, mingled with delight at England's first victory over Australia for nearly seven years. With 673 runs in the series, more than anyone on either side, he was still not only indisputably England's best player but one of the finest in the world. He was an automatic choice for England's man of the series; and his career graph showed no signs of a downturn as he entered his forties. When the capacity Oval crowd revelled in the history of his moment, a giant banner was unfurled which read: 'Well done Gooch.' It had the look of a farewell message and, indeed, many present felt they were watching his final Test innings. Others, including Gooch himself, were not so sure.

Epilogue

In the spring of 1990 an extensive book was published under the umbrella of the Test and County Cricket Board entitled *Cricket Heroes*, a number of essays on England's finest cricketers. Graham Gooch's name was not among them. This study had been planned the previous year, at a time when his Test career could have been over. The graffiti that had him coupled with a marauding Terry Alderman was not merely humorous: it was corrosive. His Test average, under 40, was not a true reflection of his ability – and he knew it. Yet what to do about this? Discontented with Test cricket and disenchanted with touring, he was on the verge of retreating into himself, his family and his county. Insecurity, the bane of his life, had resurrected itself once more.

He was then asked to captain England, to widespread astonishment. Frances Edmonds had declared of him, 'He plays cricket rather well.' Full stop. Was this a leader? He had even asked to be dropped from an England team which had become a bit of a joke. There was not much to suggest that Gooch was a deliverer, still less a Messiah. He seemed too homely, too humdrum and altogether too shy for any of that. Yet in the space of a few months he graduated from being tolerably well-known to seriously famous. He had shown that there was a place in cricket, the most esoteric of games, for perseverance and perspiration. Lugubriousness made a welcome return to fashion. In a contest dominated by psychology, he had demonstrated the supreme importance of persuading players they were capable of winning. He had become England's most successful captain since Mike Brearley, simply through having won more than he had lost. Of Gooch's contemporaries, David Gower achieved just five victories in thirty-one Tests, losing seventeen of them. England won just two of Mike Gatting's twenty-four Tests as captain. Six were lost and as many as sixteen drawn. Ten of Gower's defeats came in two series against the West Indies and Gatting had to contend with dubious umpiring in Pakistan as well as the pre-eminence of Richard Hadlee. Even so, Gooch's record of nine victories and only five defeats in twenty-three Tests as captain by the end of the 1992 series against New Zealand was a towering achievement. He, too, had to cope with the West Indies. He led England in more Tests – eight – against them than any other opposition. That the following three series against Pakistan, India and Australia were all lost was more a reflection on England's limitations and the strength of their opponents than on their increasingly weary captain.

Through his own ability, which he has maximised, and his own efforts, which have had to be considerable to overcome his sense of insecurity and the disadvantages in his background, Gooch has also become a great batsman. That is not too strong a word to bandy around. Although he came under the guidance of Bill Morris at Ilford, he never had a coach as such; nor did he benefit from the facilities that, say, his cousin Graham Saville enjoyed through growing up playing for Essex Young Amateurs. He had to overcome the humiliation of a pair on his Test début. And the steep rise in his aggregate and average at a time when many another cricketer of his generation was looking towards retirement echoed the glorious Indian summer of Tom Graveney more than two decades earlier. His eyesight should by rights have grown dim, his reflexes slowed. The opposite was the reality. And his thinking was more cogent than ever. Gooch is the consummate professional cricketer, a very different person from the batsman who regarded net practice as an exercise in belting the ball as far as possible during his early years with Essex.

Team-mates and opponents – and they, after all, should know – summarise his batsmanship as being on a par with the very best of their era. Besides, the statistics make that evident. Other than against the West Indies, Gooch's batting had evidently not reached fulfilment before he took on the England captaincy. In 66 Tests he had made 4,724 runs at 37. In 41 Tests since then he has raised his average to the mid-40s, a level comparable with Sir Colin Cowdrey and David Gower. 'Now I am a steadier, more consistent all-round player. I take fewer chances, play more percentages and am not so much of a destroyer as in the first part of my career,' was how he has summed up his batting. 'I'm proud I've been able to outlast some younger players. If anybody's going to take my place, he's going to have to play bloody well.'

Life is more straightforward for Gooch than for the likes of Cowdrey and Gower; there are few shades of grey. Gooch enjoys the riches but does not care for the limelight. He knows little of cricket records and yet was quietly pleased to make a hundred hundreds. He did not seek the England captaincy and relinquished it voluntarily, but was distraught when anything went wrong – as it did with depressing frequency from the 1992 Pakistan series onwards. He is driven much more by the prospect of fortune than by fame. He can laugh now when asked whether he will revert to the fruits of his apprenticeship when he retires from cricket. Without that drive he might have been a happier man. He would certainly have been a less effective cricketer.

Graham Gooch
Test Record to August 1993

		T	I	NO	R	HS	100s	50s	Avge
1975	v Australia	2	4	0	37	31	0	0	9.25
1978	v Pakistan	2	2	0	74	54	0	1	37.00
1978	v New Zealand	3	5	2	190	91*	0	2	63.33
1978–9	v Australia	6	11	0	246	74	0	1	22.36
1979	v India	4	5	0	207	83	0	2	41.40
1979–80	v Australia	2	4	0	172	99	0	2	43.00
1980	v India	1	2	1	57	49*	0	0	57.00
1980	v West Indies	5	10	0	394	123	1	2	39.40
1980	v Australia	1	2	0	24	16	0	0	12.00
1980–1	v West Indies	4	8	0	460	153	2	1	57.50
1981	v Australia	5	10	0	139	44	0	0	13.90
1981–2	v India	6	10	1	487	127	1	4	54.11
1982	v Sri Lanka	1	2	0	53	31	0	0	26.50
1985	v Australia	6	9	0	487	196	1	2	54.11
1985–6	v West Indies	5	10	0	276	53	0	4	27.60
1986	v India	3	6	0	175	114	1	0	29.16
1986	v New Zealand	3	5	0	268	183	1	0	53.60
1987–8	v Pakistan	3	6	0	225	93	0	2	37.50
1988	v West Indies	5	10	0	459	146	1	3	45.90
1988	v Sri Lanka	1	2	0	111	75	0	1	55.50
1989	v Australia	5	9	0	183	68	0	2	20.33
1989–90	v West Indies	2	4	1	128	84	0	1	42.66
1990	v New Zealand	3	5	0	306	154	1	1	61.20
1990	v India	3	6	0	752	333	3	2	125.33
1990–1	v Australia	4	8	0	426	117	1	4	53.25
1991	v West Indies	5	9	1	480	154*	1	2	60.00
1991	v Sri Lanka	1	2	0	212	174	1	0	106.00
1992	v New Zealand	3	5	0	161	114	1	0	32.20
1992	v Pakistan	5	8	0	384	135	1	2	48.00
1992–3	v India	2	4	0	47	18	0	0	11.75
1993	v Australia	6	12	0	673	133	2	5	56.08
Total		107	195	6	8295	333	19	45	43.87

* *not out*

Index

Also available from H. F. & G. Witherby

Great Moments in British Sport
Legendary Triumphs and Dramas Relived

Compiled and edited by
JOHN LOVESEY

Here, in words and photographs, are the moments in British sporting history that remain etched in the memory for ever, from the famous prizefight between Tom Sayers and John Heenan in 1860 to Brian Clough's dramatic resignation in 1993. In between are such legendary achievements as Fred Perry's win in the 1934 Wimbledon singles final, England's heroic regaining of the Ashes under Len Hutton in 1953, the 1966 soccer World Cup triumph and the gold medals for Coe and Ovett in the 1980 Olympics.

Over a dozen different sports are featured, with each moment vividly evoked in either a contemporary or a modern account by a leading sports writer. With its sharp, stylish writing and dramatic photographs, *Great Moments in British Sport* is the perfect gift book for all sports fans.

ISBN 0 85493 229 1   £15.99 hardback

Carling
A Man Apart

PETER BILLS

The resurgence of the England rugby union team during the last five years has been one of the great stories of modern-day sport. At the heart of that success, which has embraced Grand Slams, Triple Crowns and a World Cup Final appearance, has been Will Carling. Made captain of his country, much to his astonishment, at the age of just twenty-two, Carling quickly became one of the nation's great sporting heroes.

Yet behind the burnished public image lies an acutely sensitive, curiously vulnerable individual whose remote attitude has led some to question his approach – a factor that may have influenced the British Lions selectors when they passed him over as captain for the 1993 tour to New Zealand. For all his achievements, few have an inkling of the real Carling. There is evidence that he has always wanted it that way. But in a modern world of mass media where the game of rugby union is under the microscope as never before, can any England captain reasonably expect privacy in his chosen role? Or are the pressures on the leading players of the game which, rather absurdly, still likes to call itself amateur, simply intolerable?

In this revealing new biography Peter Bills explores the complexities and contradictions of Carling the man while chronicling his inspiring deeds for England and the Harlequins. The upshot is an illuminating, often surprising portrait of a figure who, despite – or because of – his triumphs on the field, has attracted more than his share of hostility and controversy.

ISBN 0 85493 230 5   £14.99 hardback

BETRAYAL
The Struggle for Cricket's Soul
GRAEME WRIGHT

In this brilliant, iconoclastic book Graeme Wright considers the ways in which first-class cricket has developed since 1963, when the amateur/professional distinction was introduced with the arrival of sponsorship. Asking whether the game has now betrayed its origins, with administrators selling their inheritance for the short-term, he examines in detail the problems and controversies that have bedevilled cricket in recent years. Drawing on his insider's position as former editor of *Wisden*, Graeme Wright illustrates his points through notable Test and County matches and off-field incidents, and through often surprising assessments of top players. Witty, elegant and irreverent, *Betrayal* is the most talked-about cricket book of recent years.

'Outstandingly intelligent and observant' — Christopher Martin-Jenkins, *Daily Telegraph*

'One of the most enlightened, thoughtful and disturbing books ever written on the game' — Simon Heffer, *The Spectator*

'Essential reading' — Simon Barnes, *The Times*

ISBN 0 85493 226 7   £16.99 hardback

DESMOND HAYNES
Lion of Barbados
ROB STEEN

A *Wisden* cricketer of the Year in 1990, and one of the few players to achieve 100 Test caps, Desmond Haynes is arguably the most consistent and technically accomplished opening batsman playing today. His prolific partnership with Gordon Greenidge began in 1978 and in recent years he has been a successful and immensely popular performer for Middlesex. Rob Steeen's biography, written with Haynes's full co-operation, charts his dramatic progress from an impoverished Barbados childhood to becoming a lynchpin of the all-conquering West Indies teams of the 1980s and 1990s. Haynes had been involved in many of the pivotal events in the most turbulent of cricketing eras, and the book considers such issues as intimidatory fast bowling, racism in cricket and deteriorating on-field relations. There are also shrewd appraisals of many of Haynes's team-mates and opponents, such as Viv Richards, Mike Gatting and Alan Border.

ISBN 0 85493 221 6   £16.99 hardback